The Marvelous Life of the Buddha

•

THE

MARVELOUS LIFE

OF THE

BUDDHA

Maurice Percheron

Translated by Adrienne Foulke

St Martin's Press
New York

———

•

Introduction

WESTERN MAN HAS NEVER BEEN ABLE COMPLETELY TO SATISFY his hunger to learn. He has discovered remote lands and encountered strange customs; he has assimilated manifold cultural contributions from other peoples. His social ideas have been thrown into a ferment and sometimes undermined by new ideologies. Yet he still feels a need to understand the *spirit* of other nations and peoples, and today this need is giving rise to a new humanism, a new renaissance in our Western world.

Asia is a favorite terrain in our continuing search, because, so far, we have understood it only slightly or imperfectly. We have discovered many of the riches of Asian art, philosophy, and social ideas, but the pathways of Asian thought and the meaning of its collective movements almost entirely elude us. We are disturbed to be unable to discern, much less to define, what the Asian spirit can offer us. Our growing interest in the irrational, however, is making us more and more receptive to that spirit.

Buddhism, which embraces more than five hundred million Asians, attracted only the specialists' attention until the early years of the twentieth century. Today, widely assorted ethnic and social groups in the West show a lively interest in it. This curiosity is not purely intellectual; it is related to our profound psychic disturbance. Living in a mechanized world, we look for something that lies beyond the conscious realm and speaks to something other than our rational comprehension.

When we talk about Buddhism, however, few of us can do more than conjure up notions such as total renunciation, denial of life, the search for a Nirvana that we generally—and mistakenly—take to mean nothingness, or annihilation. Furthermore, we tend to think of Buddhism merely as a hermetic religious movement. As heirs to the clear linear thought of the Greeks, we find it difficult to see a priori that another kind of logic, expressed by indirection and by symbolism, may exist. We are not easily moved by an austere philosophy that proposes the impermanence of all things and teaches that human actions have inescapable consequences. For lack of the necessary key, we cannot conceive that there may be ways to escape from human suffering. We do not concede that total responsibility (responsibility without qualification or evasion) is granted to each individual in a life process whereby the effects of his own behavior determine, for better or for worse, his own salvation.

Buddhism confronts us with a bewildering array of jurisdictions, sects, monastic orders, and rites that vary from country to country. Like all religious movements, it is related to a moral and mystical code of behavior. But does this mean that Buddhism is really a religion? If we allow the term at all, we must qualify it by saying that Buddhism is a religion only on the surface.

We should remember that the Buddhism of today is the result of centuries of exuberant growth, elaboration, and modification. The original teachings actually denied all theology, all dogma, and even the idea of divinity. The basis of Buddhism is anything but religious.

The Buddha was wise enough, however, to understand that he could not completely alter ideas that had been in circulation for thousands of years. Furthermore, he saw nothing amiss in man's continuing to honor the gods. ("All gods are good, provided one pray to them with a pure heart.") He did, however, insist that the gods had no power over the happiness or misery of mankind. ("Have the gods ever spared you sickness, old age, and death?") He was essentially a positivist in thought—as he was positive in action—and directed his energies toward combating the obscurantism of the Brahmans and their stranglehold over the people, not toward repudiating divinities.

One still finds, in the various sects, the essence of his original Doctrine. It is manifest in a certain attitude of the individual toward himself and toward the world. It is profoundly rationalistic; it acknowledges no divine revelation; it sanctions no initiation ritual nor does it prescribe any practices that, in effect, limit eligibility for or membership in a sectarian group. A Buddhist is simply a person who acts, in all things and in all circumstances, in accordance with the Doctrine of Buddha.

This is the heart of the matter. The core of Buddhism has not changed, even if books of revelation and elaborate rituals have been added. The great teachers who have been responsible for these developments have probably made Buddhism more precise and complete in relation to the original concept. Their writings clarify the individual's psychological attitude toward sensory data; they teach unconditional practice of non-violence; respect for an equality that derives from the simple fact of existence; rejection of force in settling both personal quarrels and the fate of groups; denial of all racial differences, caste divisions, or competitive faiths. The social basis of Buddhism, indeed, is unqualified tolerance. In a world where we speak all too easily of conflict and war, we would be wrong to disregard this.

Who was this Buddha, whose message has so deeply stirred Asia that almost half the continent accepts it? First of all, he was not a mythical figure—no matter how unreal an appearance he has been given in the various art representations of him that range from the tormented Tibetan paintings to the admirable Indian and Khmer sculptures to the familiar porcelain figurine with its bulging paunch.

The Buddha actually existed; he is as historically real as Rameses II, Plato, or Alexander the Great. He is one of the very few people of whom ancient India has bequeathed us some account, chiefly in the form of legends that grew up around him in the centuries following his sojourn on earth.

These legends are wrought of a fusion of Indian beliefs that predated him, actual facts, and teachings that he or his followers unquestionably preached. A wealth of the miraculous and poetic detail that so delights Indian taste was woven into his history, although the man's life was one of exceptional simplicity and his own words emphasized his unyielding rationalism.

The Buddha—called, variously, the Perfect One, Bhagavat, Shakyamuni, or the Wise One of the Shakyas—never claimed to be divine; he promulgated no heresies; he did not even benefit from the glory of martyrdom. Insofar as doctrine is concerned, he cannot even be called a reformer. What Shakyamuni did was to give expression to an impulse that was already latent throughout the peninsula but which the Brahman caste was smothering in paralyzing ritual.

He did not challenge the ancient methods that India had set up whereby the individual won salvation after death. Instead, as his point of departure he took unformulated ideas from earlier times; from the deeper layers of the psyche he extracted primordial, forgotten concepts; rejecting the miraculous and subjecting every affirmation to a pitiless critique, he sought, found, and offered a different way to salvation. If his teachings cannot be called revolutionary, certainly he himself needed rare spiritual strength to dare clear away the Brahmanic underbrush of complicated rites, quasi-magic, and sacrifices that made the gods themselves the slaves of the officiating priest.

In the Indian world, excess seems always to have been the rule. No asceticism was ever sufficiently severe. The vital bodily functions and the mental faculties had to be reduced to near extinction, to a kind of living death; this had seemed the best path to follow for the soul to escape further transmigrations and to melt into the universal unity. Sacrificial rites had multiplied, gesture had acquired capital importance. The fear of defilement had become a devouring anxiety that hung over every waking and sleeping moment, over conscience, speech, and the most trivial deed, over the shadow of the body and even over the innermost recesses of the soul. The people were at once the masters and slaves of innumerable gods—they being the thousand facets of a single diamond. The priestly caste devoted all its energies to speculation, until the Brahman could maneuver with prodigious ease through the inextricable coils of his own complex concepts.

The Buddha brushed aside such questions as "Where does

man come from?" or "Why is man?" to ask the one question that to him had value: "What is this soul which man claims is eternal?" He transcended moldy beliefs, side-stepped the seven hundred and eighty billion divinities, and returned to essentials.

To come back to the historical character of the Buddha: he belonged to the Gautama family, nobles of the Kshatriya, or warrior caste, who lived in northwest India, between the Ganges and the Himalayas. The Gautamas were rulers of the Shakya clan; as such, they were princelings and great land-owners who lived as the vassals of more powerful sovereigns.

The child was born between 544 and 556 B.C., and legend has it that his was a miraculous birth, his mother Maya having conceived while a virgin. As a natural corollary, he came into the world unblemished and pure; he both walked and talked in the first few minutes of life, thereby affirming his future dominion over the entire world. Thirty-two signs of predestination marked him from that moment.

In his early years, he lived the carefree idle existence of a young prince, excelling his noble companions in intelligence and intuitive understanding, and in physical strength and dexterity. He married a ravishingly beautiful princess with whom he lived, in a fairy-like palace, for a brief period of idyllic happiness. However, while walking through the capital city, he saw an old man, a sick man, and a corpse being borne to the funeral pyre, and he became deeply troubled by human suffering. A conversation with a wandering monk made him realize that he had a mission, that he had been called to free mankind from the pain which illness, decay, age, and death bring.

He loved his young wife tenderly, yet he gave up a life of happiness and set out on his own, not like a prince but like the most humble Untouchable. In order to seek the Truth, he became a wandering monk and followed the ascetic teachings of the yogis who lived as hermits in the forests of the Ganges valley; in the snows of the Himalayas he himself practiced asceticism until he nearly died of tuberculosis.

This experience was a spiritual disillusionment, and it was only after years of further wandering and fruitless striving that he attained a revelation of the laws that govern the course of the world and acquired knowledge of all things. This is known as his Illumination, and it took place one night while he was sitting in a state of ecstasy at the foot of a fig tree.

He perceived that the heavy toll demanded of man—the anguish that grips everyone, whether or not he recognizes it —is the profound anxiety man feels before both life and death, and he saw, further, that this anxiety has clearly defined causes.

First, there is desire, the frantic craving to live, to possess, to get ahead. This is the egoistic desire that hardens a man and makes him indifferent to others. Later, the Wise One symbolized it in the green serpent of sensuality.

Then there is non-mastery of self, the failure of man's will and of his highest aspirations before the intense drive of his passions; this is lack of control, or the spirit of vengeance. Gautama evoked it in the red turkey cock of anger.

Lastly, he perceived that the third cause of human suffering is ignorance. By ignorance the Buddha meant to mistake one's own nature; to let oneself be trapped by appearances; to believe in the permanence of self, of other beings, and of things; to mistake illusion for reality; willfully to ignore the fact that cosmic laws regulate the course of the universe. Such ignorance reduces a human being to the level of a swine.

What the Buddha understood through his Illumination under the bodhi tree of Buddh Gaya and what he later taught is this: all beings that compose the universe are identical in essence. All are animated by the same principle of life that manifests itself in a thousand forms throughout the phenomenal order. In a word, all are attached, individually and en masse, to a wheel of evolution; the strivings of each are variously resolved, but that resolution leaves the imprint of its power and direction on the entire universe.

Our actions are linked together; they follow one upon another, and they follow us as well. Fortified by repetition, they influence behavior; insensibly, they modify character, personality, and even the body. A good action makes us better; a bad action degrades us. And so we experience joy or suffering, reward or punishment—in either case, we receive our just deserts.

But our life runs too short a span for us fully to settle our accounts. The disturbances our deeds have caused do not cease with our death. No redemption is possible, and they have repercussions that assume their full dimensions as the years pass. The actions of each of us vibrate along a chain, from generation to generation, without end. Thus there exists in the world not only homogeneity of essence but an inescapable linking together of seemingly separate parts.

Shakyamuni did accept the concept of rebirth. In the course of successive transmigrations a physical vehicle is provided for the irreducible core of psychic energy that every living thing possesses. (This is not what we call a soul; he thought the soul flawed with impermanence.) No being is born that does not die and transmigrate. The physical shell or envelope of the living thing is mortal, but the psychic energy cannot be destroyed and it continues to be reincarnated. It will find itself in a better or worse condition, according to the meritorious acts or the errors committed in the preceding life.

The Buddha himself symbolized these implacable transmigrations, this fluctuation of rebirths, as the Wheel of Life.

Eternally repeating the same phases, every living creature rotates around this Wheel, the spokes of which embrace the divine, human, animal, and infernal worlds.

When death comes, the errors that man or dog has been guilty of—each, naturally, on his own scale and in relation to the ideal line of conduct for his own species—will have their irredeemable repercussions in the transmigration to come. This is the Law of Karma. Memory does not survive from one existence into the next but the burden of what has taken place in a previous life does, and it can be neither lifted nor expiated.

The man who voluntarily seeks death will not thereby have delivered himself from suffering. The suicide's karma would require his completing the transmigrations imposed upon him and, in addition, he would have to atone for his cowardice in having swerved from the right way of life. The terminal point to be achieved at the end of innumerable lives is no longer to be reborn; this is not the same thing as to live no longer.

The human being's possibility of ascending to a life one degree more evolved than the preceding is determined solely by elementary rules of conduct based on truth, understanding, and compassion for all living things—in a word, on goodness. Man shall practice tolerance; he shall have an open mind; he shall prove himself imbued with the idea of equality. He shall also demonstrate total mastery of self. This last does not mean renunciation; the "average" man is meant to live an ordinary human existence. The whole point is that he live it according to the highest standard possible. To the monk alone is reserved, through total comprehension of the Doctrine, accession to the pure regions of contact with the Absolute.

If every transgression an individual commits disturbs his development in his current existence and has repercussions in what will follow after his brief earthly passage, it also affects evolution in general and influences future generations. These suffer from such pre-fixed degeneration just as they profit from improvements effected through the good behavior of each being that has preceded them.

The idea of transmigration, then, assumes all the force implicit in the bequeathing or receiving of a heritage. The Buddha's doctrine extends beyond the individual scope to emphasize that we are all, consciously or unconsciously, associated in a common destiny. We can achieve the infinite blessedness that Perfect Knowledge brings only by bearing our own small stone to the edifice of universal well-being. Metaphysics, morality, and sociology join, in this way, to resolve the problem of evil and to eliminate suffering.

No one has ever revealed foundations for personal and social morality more unshakable than this implacable connection between our own actions and their consequences. "What has happened cannot not have happened."

When the Buddha placed responsibility squarely on the individual for assuring his own spiritual health—and in so doing distinguished him from the collective as well as from the divine—he also energetically emphasized that what is called "I" is as impermanent as the body. At no moment is a human being identical to what he was a second earlier, or to what he will be a second later. A given state of being derives from the preceding state but also differs from it. The one constant that the human being can discover is identification with Brahman, the World Soul or Universal Essence. He will achieve this only when he is able to avoid the snares of sensations, when he stops pridefully imagining that he is a distinct personality, and recognizes the reality of the total void, i.e., that he exists in the midst of nothingness.

Mystical experience or ecstasy leads to such Supreme

Knowledge. The Buddha himself achieved this after his karma had been subjected to countless rebirths, the interminable cycle of which he relived at the time of his Illumination. From that moment, he was worthy of Nirvana—that is, of no longer having to be reborn after his final earthly sojourn and with his mission of salvation accomplished.

These all too sketchy remarks indicate that Nirvana is not death. The living being is only an impermanent collection of ephemeral elements; he vanishes when the thing that has caused these elements to cohere has itself disappeared. This thing is desire. We cannot say that a being has been annihilated if it has sustained an illusion of identity only because a cohesive force held its constituent elements together. When the cause disappears, the effect simply stops—just as the light goes out when the electric current is shut off.

Accordingly, we cannot speak of the death of the Perfect One. He himself indicated very precisely that the "I" his disciples might have considered fixed and stable was only a continual mobility. Nothing of that which exists has been created out of nothingness and so cannot return to nothingness. On the other hand, the law of causality and the law of interdependent origins impose perpetual transformations.

The Buddha wished to make these great but as yet unperceived truths known to his contemporaries. Long before the many others who were to say the same, he declared that struggle and suffering are universal. He discovered the continuousness of energy, and he verified cosmic unity in both time and space. To people ignorant of logic and synthesis, he taught the laws of evolution and of cause and effect.

Having demonstrated the causes of suffering, he sought for a remedy. He did not find it in any inaccessible heaven but in man himself, in his actions and thoughts, which have irreparable and everlasting effects. From such firm bases he taught that evil will diminish only through an increase in knowledge, through altruism, and human solidarity. The acknowledgment of universal homogeneity, of the constitutional kinship of all beings, of a basic identity—this is the source of all altruism, of all "socialism," in which human beings recognize that they are brothers to everything that lives in Nature. For a Buddhist, a gnat and a buffalo and a man are subject to the same laws of existence; they possess a comparable nature and identical potentialities. They merely exist on different levels of development and growth.

Another of Gautama's great accomplishments was his daring challenge of social forms that had inhibited free thought, and his clarifying, liberating, and enlarging concepts of universal unity.

To a society that was living without hope under the burden of caste divisions, the whims of powerful lords, and the despotism of the Brahmans, Shakyamuni brought freedom of thought and the concept of a love that is extended to all living things. To an elite, independent enough to dare disregard conformism, he offered a method of developing the inner life that can deliver man from temporal insecurity and even from death. Lastly, to those who had attained the level of "disinterested, impersonal and universal thought" he revealed a world that is eternal and single in essence. He charged this elect, capable of the loftiest comprehension, with the responsibility of helping others to reach the supreme goal—Knowledge.

The Perfect One never doubted that the individual can transform his nature; he conceived of this as being possible through the careful cultivation of the germ of "good" that exists in every being. Man must seek to develop his latent potentialities, for perfectibility cannot be spontaneous. The Buddhist does not believe in such a thing as Efficient Grace; within himself the human being must find his master and his guide. Buddhist instruction is like a succession of arrows pointing the way; meditation and discipline are only tools.

When the Buddha teaches us not to cause any living thing—no matter how lowly—to suffer, and not to seize another's property, and to resist the enslavements of the flesh, he is not satisfied simply to say, "Thou shalt not kill. . . . Thou shalt not bear false witness. . . ." He means this: "Thou shalt free thyself in thy innermost being of every attitude that expresses anger, spite, greed or concupiscence toward thy neighbor." This is very different from external conformity to sound moral principles; it is a question of inner purification.

Shakyamuni went still further, attaching primary importance to the spirit of love, which he placed even above good deeds. Good deeds "are not worth a sixteenth part of that love that frees the heart." Charity? Yes. Compassion? Still better. But "the love that shines, illumines, and irradiates" ennobles the human being and lends beauty to the many hard lives man must experience before he need no longer be reborn.

By teaching rules of individual moral conduct that could effect a perceptible improvement also in communal life, by preaching compassion and the absolute equality of all living things, he struck telling blows to the social stratification that had characterized millenia of human life. Man was rescued from suffocation in the familial and tribal collectivity, and assumed his proper status and value as an individual. It can safely be claimed that Buddhism was the most important social phenomenon that happened in India before Independence.

So profound a rupture with Indian sociology was, nevertheless, the weak point in early Buddhism. The vigor of age-old social organizations eventually left Buddhism with no alternatives but to surrender to the resurgent influence of Brahmanism or to allow itself to be transformed by absorbing certain earlier local myths. The latter happened, most notably, in Tibet.

This retreat before the power of the Trimurti (the Hindu divine trinity of Brahma, Vishnu, and Siva) and this adaptation to deistic ideas that the Buddha himself had condemned were regressions, and they were facilitated by the fact that the Perfect One never wrote down or dictated his teachings. Shakyamuni preached and expressed his ideas figuratively, so that his lofty truths could be grasped by the masses. He used illustrations and imagery that the imagination and heart of the people quickly seized on—and presently transformed into legends. Ananda, his favorite disciple (a counterpart, perhaps, of Saint John), tells us that the Doctrine can be understood only if one listens, eyes closed, without trying to analyze or discuss it, and if one allows the words to set chords vibrating that have never been touched before. Did not Gautama say "One must speak with silence"? And did Ananda not add "How does one evoke by word or letter a subtle perfume, the blue of the morning sky, or a harmony of the harp"?

Famous scholars such as Kashyapa, Nagarjuna, and Asanga later gave form to what the Perfect One had said or outlined. The thousands of books on Buddhism, produced through the centuries, have, little by little, cramped the Buddha's teaching within rigid explications. What should touch the listener's heart has now become dogma, complicated and difficult to penetrate, the more devitalized for having been minutely dissected in order to eliminate obscurities, imprecisions, and contradictions that defy synthesis.

The masses are not to be persuaded by such intellectual exercises. Human beings generally relish the miraculous and India, in particular, has lived throughout the ages on such intimate terms with its gods that, inevitably, the message of the

Buddha has been profoundly altered by popular manipulation. For example, as the authentic teachings of the Perfect One became blurred, the masses' appetite for the extraordinary conferred divine origin on him. The faithful came to see Prince Siddhartha Gautama, of the noble clan of the Shakyas, as the last incarnation of one of those bodhisattvas who, after an interminable succession of existences replete with charity and serene devotion, have deserved to attain Wisdom. For mankind, a bodhisattva is both the example of what every living thing can hope to become and the source of help given to those who pray for it. The bodhisattva is freed of all passion and has only one lap of the journey to complete. Near the Guardians of the Universe, he awaits the hour of his final rebirth, when he will acquire Absolute Knowledge and, by experiencing Illumination, become a Buddha, or an Enlightened One.

For more than twenty centuries, Gautama has been revered by Asians as a bodhisattva who was incarnated in a man and who descended to earth to attain knowledge of all things. Having found Perfect Wisdom through his Illumination, he dedicated his human days to delivering the world of the anguish that enchains it. Then, his work done, he entered Nirvana, the ineffable kingdom of the cessation of desire, of the freedom from rebirth.

With time, two great schools of Buddhism came into existence, and each proliferated into numerous sects. The first is called, variously, the Hinayana (Lesser Vehicle), or Theravada (the Way of the Elders), or simply the Southern School by virtue of the people who follow it—Singhalese, Burmese, Laotians, Cambodians, and Siamese. The Theravada School aims to respect the original teachings of the Master; it considers the Buddha to have been a mortal man, a sage whose Illumination made him superior to other men. His Nirvana is stripped of any divine nature; everyone can achieve the same by submitting to monastic discipline. Nirvana represents the desired end of a destiny that is determined solely by actions performed in the course of more and more nearly pure existences.

The Mahayana (Greater Vehicle) School, or the Northern School, which is followed in Tibet and China, does not make salvation contingent on monastic status. Not only humans but all sentient beings, no matter how inferior, can become buddhas—in the sense that the buddhistic nature is latent in them. If he seeks it, every man can attain buddhahood in his lifetime through his love for the bodhisattvas and the buddhas of the past, by sacrificing his personal needs to theirs, and by practicing a compassionate charity. Once he has become a bodhisattva, he will be able to intervene, in his turn, to assist in the salvation of others.

In Mahayana Buddhism, Shakyamuni the Enlightened One loses his historical character. He gives way to a pantheon of buddhas, who are considered redeemers and are endowed with divinity. Each of these fully consummated buddhas dwells in paradise, in the midst of bodhisattvas, or future buddhas, who have taken an oath not to enter Nirvana before they have labored to lead all living creatures to the same goal.

The peaks of intellectual, moral, psychological, and spiritual achievement that the individual can reach, through personal efforts alone, are so lofty that he who attains them has become as different from ordinary men as the latter are from animals. But what has been attained by one can be attained by all; this is the sense of the expression "Greater Vehicle."

Underlying all the rites, accompanying all the speculation, behind all the prayers, beyond all heavens and hells that have been elaborated (all things, it will be remembered, that the Perfect One had rejected), are to be found the fudamental concepts: the non-ego, impermanence, the illusory nature of what our senses teach us. An indestructible kernel of Doctrine persists under all the religious forms. The Buddha brought to humanity such a concept of the world and of the role the individual plays in the march of the universe that, no matter what emotional overlays have been added, his words cannot be smothered.

When the Buddhistic teachings broke away from local ideas and influences, they spread, conquering as well as being conquered, throughout Asia. Now, by roundabout ways, they come to speak intimately to us in the West. The white man, warned by science that the senses offer us illusions, and influenced by psychological ideas such as those of Jung, is ready to understand the meaning of Buddhism and to benefit from the power with which the Perfect One imbued his Law.

Almost twenty-five hundred years ago, the Buddha understood that man has one vision of the universe through the medium of the senses; still another if he detaches himself from sensory impressions; and another still if, beyond his perception of general laws that govern the cosmic equilibrium, he reaches the realm of the absolute, which is inaccessible to intellection.

The most astonishing thing for the modern man who studies the Perfect One's ideas is to recognize in them the germ of the most advanced concepts in the fields of atomic physics and analytical psychology.

Mathematics now attests to the fact that, whereas our senses convey notions of substance, form, and color, nothing exists in reality except occurrences in time and space; that is, nothing exists but forces subject to a constantly varying flux that determines varying equilibriums. Every material object is nothing more than an immense space meagerly inhabited by atoms separated by distances that, compared with their own size, are prodigious. And these atoms themselves are only magnetic fields, condensations of energy subject to perpetual shifts of intensity, to constantly changing attractions and repulsions that destroy one equilibrium in order immediately to establish another.

A kind of new "mathematical legality" has been created and verified by results in which, apparently, the observer does not participate. Deliberately detaching himself from the rational, he proceeds across unexplored terrains, unflinchingly employing imaginary numbers and fractional exponents, referring to curved universes, to gradients of energy—all of these being notions that defy a logic built upon the perfect functioning of the senses and of reason.

The most recent concepts of the atom have even shown that the instantaneous and unceasing transformations of these quanta of energy are subject to formal laws only when a large number of them are involved; the isolated atom obeys only the law of variability.

The illusory nature of all sensory perception . . . impermanence . . . are these not the two solid pillars of Buddhism? Our modern scientist cannot even know whether the new immaterial world of which he has a certain presentiment is real or not, for, after all, the mathematical physics that supplies its coördinates is again a product of the mind.

Thus, the very point that Buddha dared confront is being scientifically developed; that is, the absolute impossibility for the intelligence to judge whether what it perceives or conceives is valid; for the subject to separate itself from an object that is its own creation. No more than the knife can sever its own blade can the brain observe its own functioning.

This doubt about what we actually know has led scientific thinkers to another characteristically Buddhistic insight; that is, awareness of the relativity of reality. We can pass beyond the limitations imposed by the subject-object confusion only via escape into the irrational on a transcendental plane that is disengaged from logical causalities. Here we move in an extrasensory world that, a priori, is certainly no more infected with illusion than is the world of sensations.

An identical junction can be envisaged with still another science—psychology as formulated by William James, with his discontinuous moment-points, or as conceived today by Jung. A perpetual state of flux exists in the interplay between the personal conscious and unconscious and the collective archetypal unconscious, in the coexistence of contrary impulses, in the interaction of all known and unknown psychological quantities in mental or emotional impressions, cognitions, and conflicts. This, briefly, postulates a series of psychological equilibriums that have no more determining causality than do atoms.

Personality then appears in its true light: unstable, impermanent, fluid; it is governed by temporary combinations, eludes all control, and depends, more or less, on circumstances, acts, and thoughts that have been slightly or not at all apprehended.

The "I" and the atom reflect equally well the anarchic state that lies beyond the phenomenal perception of time and space such as the Buddha proposed. One can only be astounded by the prescience of this man who eclipsed all limits of time and place. And it is understandable why the Western world is beginning to divine that the Doctrine, despite the modifications it has undergone, embraces perhaps one of the supreme treasures of humanity.

This brief account of the Doctrine makes it possible to wander now through the marvelous garden of legend, with little risk that its often heady perfume will distort an understanding of the Buddha's ideas.

The following story of the Buddha draws directly on the Indian "Lalita Vistara" and the Tibetan "Rgya tch'er rol pa." It may surprise some readers to find it crowded with the gods of India whom the Buddha seemed to care nothing about. One or another mythological figure, undeniably anthropomorphic, is always turning up in the miraculous life of the Illumined One. Even Indians most attached to the Doctrine have not repudiated Brahma, Siva, and Vishnu. While the Perfect One denied that any god intervenes in the affairs of men and clearly stated that man is born alone, lives alone, and dies alone, he allowed that "All gods are good, provided one pray to them with a pure heart" and so left open a door to the Seven Heavens.

Essentially, myth is not an invention, not an enchanting fairy tale men regale each other with; it is a psychological reality. It is a living truth that relates to periods when men neglected to record their history in writing, and it continues to influence the destinies of the world, now and in the future.

Mythology is replete with imagery that evokes the earliest feelings of the peoples of antiquity, feelings that may even have predated human history and that subsequently became the common heritage of all men, irrespective of period or race. It is an eternal rejuvenating sap and helps to explain why the marvelous life of the Buddha can touch a Westerner no less that a Chinese or Indian in his inmost self. And so we will see Agni the Fire God, and Indra, and Ushas or Goddess of the Dawn—indeed, all divinities—gather respectfully around to defend and support the message of Gautama Shakyamuni, who was enlightened by Perfect Knowledge.

Book One

I

ONE DAY—NOT AN EARTHLY BUT A DIVINE DAY THAT IS MEAS-
ured by who knows how many hundreds of years—the
thirty-three gods of India gathered together in their paradise
for a conference.

The Buddha himself never mentioned this meeting,
which took place some twenty-five hundred years ago. But
men have told about it ever since in such minute detail that it
must indeed have happened, and the account that we will
faithfully pass on now is theirs.

However, before we slip into the divine council room to
eavesdrop as the Thirty-three debate, we should arm ourselves with a map of celestial geography. It includes so many

paradises, one superimposed upon another into infinity, that one runs the risk of getting lost. There is, for example, the Lofty Dwelling of Pure Light, where Adi-Buddha meditates; there is the unimaginable Supreme Region of forms freed of sensuality, where sixteen firmaments are tiered in four spheres of contemplation; there is the lower Region of Desires, where the seven hundred and eighty billion gods have arranged for themselves, in hierarchic order, six heavens that, as everyone must know, rest on piles above our earth. And there are many other domains, reserved variously for spirits, heavenly dancers, musicians, and for the troops charged with the defense of these assorted empyreans.

From all these manifold worlds that circulate in the sky no sound—not even sounds made by the gods—reaches the indescribable Lofty Dwelling. There, in perfect solitude, palpitates Essential Wisdom, or Supreme Knowledge—Primordial Thought, in a word, which exists of itself, with neither beginning nor end. Nothing has ever disturbed Primordial Thought; nothing matters to it, not even the five Dhyani Buddhas, the "Meditating Enlightened Ones," who are reflections of its motionless Wisdom.

There are five of these heavenly Conquerors, just as there are five senses, five virtues, five sacred colors, and five cardinal points of the compass over which they reign in silence. Five is a sacred figure, the number that stands for the marriage between heaven and earth, the union between that which unchangingly *is* and the bustle of rebirths that engages human and non-human creatures alike.

Astride his elephant, Akshobhya, who is all blue, watches over the east, a lotus in his hand. Yellow as the marigold, Ratnasambhava guards the south, while Amogha-Siddhi, the color of emeralds, protects the north. As the sun hastens toward its setting in the west, it is awaited by Amitabha, the Purple One. And in the center, above the zenith and the nadir, reigns Vairochana, blinding to behold in his immaculate whiteness.

These five Buddhas of Meditation, whom people grandly call Jinas, or Conquerors, are distinct from each other, but, rather like the whisperings of the wind, they are also united. In their indissoluble union is forged the first link of an endless chain that leads from Adi-Buddha to the universe, that joins the One to the many, the irrational to the material (which is a product of the mind), and the unchangeable to that which is incessantly changing and perpetually evolving.

The eternal, wordless contemplation of the Jinas requires an active counterpart, and each of the five Meditating Ones is twinned to a kind of double, a buddha of action. Men have never dared attribute forms or features to the Uncreated Supreme, but they have pictured the Jinas as humble monks who sit in unseeing contemplation of their begging bowls, and have adorned their active reflections with crowns and precious jewels. One must not mistake the nature of these doubles, however. They are not sons or younger brothers of the five motionless Jinas; they are actually the Dhyani Buddhas themselves, in glory and action without end.

The most glittering of them all is Amitayus, who is the image incarnate of Amitabha's Boundless Light. Amitayus wears thirteen jewels, such as no earthly craftsman could dream of copying; he holds in his hand the cup filled with the ambrosia of everlasting life. The gods are most deferential toward him, for he has the power to release them, if he wishes, from the cycle of rebirths to which, even as gods, they remain subject.

Side by side with the humble and the radiant Buddhas, the bodhisattvas peacefully meditate. We might call them archangels. These are Buddha-aspirants, who have lived an incalculable number of existences not only on earth but also on the habitable stars. They have been, variously, men or women, animals, plants, wind or bubbling spring; they have lived now at the top of the ladder of reasoning beings, now at the bottom. Little by little, in the course of their manifold lives, they have drawn nearer Supreme Wisdom; slowly they have learned the cause of all things, and expiated the errors they committed when they existed in lower forms. Now they must once more—and for the last time—cross the tumultuous river of life to reach the farther bank, where, having known all, learned all, understood all, they will no longer need to be born again.

They will then be able to enter the heaven of Practical Wisdom and become Enlightened Ones; that is, completed buddhas who, by their virtue, perfect knowledge, and renunciation of all desire, have entered the peace of Nirvana, the peace of Non-being.

As they await this glorious moment, the bodhisattvas also reflect the creative spirit of the five Jinas. They may be assigned to serve as heavenly messengers or as troops to fight the demons of air and earth; in so doing, the bodhisattvas function simply as the active power of meditation. In turn, they are assisted in their work by earthly reflections or doubles of their own, who have attained or will attain Illumination here below.

For example, Amitabha, Boundless Light and Guardian of the West, invested his active function in the Bodhisattva Avalokiteshvara, whom men call the Compassionate One. Twenty-five hundred years ago, this archangel of the merciful heart had to be made incarnate in a man in order to complete his last required earthly existence. As our story will tell, he appeared in India, in the guise of one Prince Siddhartha, who became the monk Gautama, and whom men have since called the Buddha, the Enlightened One, the Perfect One, Shakyamuni or Sage of the Shakyas, and many other names.

Thousands upon thousands upon thousands of bodhisatt-vas are awaiting the hour when, in one world or another, they will live their last life, devoting it to the salvation of others. However, the universe is so vast that our own planet has known only four such buddhas, and it will have to wait eighty thousand years before another is incarnated in a man. He will be called Maitreya, and he will represent on earth the Bodhisattva Visvapani, who is, in turn, the active agent of Amogha-Siddhi, Jina of the North. Impatient mankind has already dubbed him "He who will come" or "The Golden Messiah."

There is not the slightest difference between those bo-dhisattvas who are emanations of the five Jinas and the others. All are robed like princes and glitter with jewels. All are beings of compassion and kindness; all have postponed enter-ing Nirvana in order to help mankind. Palaces of crystal shelter the radiant grace of their perennial youth, and every benevolent gesture they make is accompanied by a shower of blossoms and heavenly music.

One can easily go astray in this kingdom of Practical Wisdom. There are so many buddhas and bodhisattvas! When Shakyamuni came down to earth to teach men, he—in-tentionally, no doubt—omitted any mention of the thirty-five buddhas who are assigned to hear confession, or the seven healing buddhas, or the female counterparts of the bodhisatt-vas, and a great many others, some of whom know how to conceal their beneficent nature behind the masks of devils. His silence on such points has given rise to the claim that he did not believe in them.

Fortunately for us, in the intervening two thousand years others have been more communicative, although what they have related is all too little—or too much.

Some men have been able to tell us of these admirably ordered heavens because they have known the mystical experience of ecstasy. They did not actually enter a heaven; if they had, they would not have become humans beings once more, after regaining normal consciousness. But they had fleeting visions of these regions, such as one might have through a half-open door, lasting the flick of an eyelash. If they can evoke the Region of Pure Spirit for us, it is because they have been dazzled by an unendurable brightness. When they tell us of the Region of Forms freed of sensuality, we must suppose that their mystical seizure conferred prodigiously sharp sight on their closed eyes. The lower Region of Desire is more accessible, and perhaps its portals did momentarily swing open on the sixfold domain of the gods— the six devalokas, as we call them.

However we interpret their experience, we should listen with forbearance to what these ascetics tell us they have seen. Some All-Powerful One may have revealed himself with particular clarity to a favorite monk. Perhaps his glimpse of the assembled gods so disconcerted him that he became confused, and fabricated a detail or two as he strove to reassemble his conflicting recollections. None of this really matters. The truth is surely even more beautiful than any account he could give of his vison.

Ordinarily, perfect calm reigned in the paradise of the thirty-three gods, but on this particular day, which was to become memorable in human history, they managed to create quite a stir of excitement. They were listening to the Bodhisattva Avalokiteshvara, who had come down among them. They were listening to him with their hearts, that is, for in these heavens words are not needed to convey thought.

"O Amitabha," he was saying, "thou from whom I issue, O Boundless Light, guide me now as I descend to earth once more. Grant me the strength to be pure enough in this new earthly life that it may be my last and that I, bathed in everlasting and golden clarity, may finally enter thy kingdom of the West and a Nirvana without end."

Secure in his knowledge of the way that leads to deliverance, gentle and compassionate, clairvoyant and firm of purpose, free of pride, fear or envy, the Bodhisattva concluded, "My hour has come. My reflection must go down into the world of men and teach them how to free themselves from suffering."

The gods were aglow with pride to be witnessing such an event as this. For it must be understood that the Thirty-three were Brahmanic deities, and as such they had suffered a kind of celestial demotion. Once they had been supreme, but they had been slow to realize that metaphysical powers exist far more potent than they. With time, they had been relegated to a lower rank in heaven and now, no more than kings without crowns, they were reduced to silent, submissive veneration of the five Conquerors. On earth, however, they were still fervently worshiped, for no human being suspected there had been any such upheaval until the time came for the marvelous story of the Buddha to be written.

As gods they were still superior to mortal men, of course; their temperament was more defined and their feelings were more clearly differentiated. They were less subject to suffering than men, and they also enjoyed a million times longer life. Nonetheless, they were afflicted to the bottom of their beings to know that their lofty condition did not protect them against old age and death, or even against a possible lowering of status in their rebirth. They dreaded the possibility that they might be condemned to live the next life in one of the several purgatories and be tormented by fire or ice or insatiable hunger and thirst. Or a human body might provide shelter for their essence. After such joy as they had known as gods, they still might have to experience all human cares again, and face the prospect of being reborn in a still worse condition.

However, all such agitating thoughts seemed to be suspended as the Thirty-three listened to the Bodhisattva. The birds perching in the tree that grants every wish had fallen silent; the chattering goddesses had become mute. Siva glanced with something like conspiratorial amusement at his wife and even she, Durga the Terrible, was smiling. Vishnu turned more transparently blue than usual, which heightened the rose in the cheeks of his ravishing wife Lakshmi, and the green in the face of his second spouse, Bhumi. The Nagas coiled themselves trustingly beside Garuda, although the bird was their sworn enemy. The kunnaris had lowered their eight-holed flutes and did not even brush the strings of their lutes; the Apsarases had stopped their dancing and were standing motionless, one arm gracefully poised in the air. Rudra quite forgot to bellow like an angry sea lion. And so for them all, except Indra, who never once lowered the flagon of soma from his lips.

When the Bodhisattva had finished speaking, the entire assembly fell to discussing the time and place for his rebirth. Of all the countries in the world, the land of the rose-apple, which extends from the Ganges to the Indus, seemed most suitable. For the date, the Bodhisattva himself chose the year 544 B.C., and for the locality, the town of Kapilavastu, in the valley of the Ganges; he decided, furthermore, to be the spirit of the eldest son born to the king of the Shakyas.

"No doubt," Brahma let fall from the height of his zenith, "no doubt that's a sound choice. Kapilavastu is a prosperous town, it's a delightful town. King Suddhodano comes from unusually good stock. And he's a distinguished man, very rich—" He noticed that the gods were listening closely and warmed to his subject. "As for his wife, she is the purest of women. She is an illusion, a dream of beauty—which is why she was named Maya Devi, of course, after the goddess who tempts men and gods alike. She is in the flower of her youth, and she's not yet had a child."

Everyone leaned forward to catch what Siva was muttering to himself.

"She's had no chance to have a child," the Hairy One growled in his scarlet throat. "She took my yogis' vow of chastity, you know. She's his wife in name only."

"What does that matter! She will be a mother just the same! She is slim, but her body is strong as a diamond. Her spirit is as pure—"

Indra brusquely interrupted the Protector of Men to continue with a eulogy warmed by soma. "Her belly is curved like a bow and her navel is deep. Her face glows with laughter under hair dusky as the black bee. Her eyes are as clear as the fresh petal of the lotus, her teeth white as a cluster of jasmine. Never have her lovely eyebrows frowned. Her voice is as gentle as her nature. She is just, modest, sincere. . . . There is no one like her. . . . So," he tilted his flagon, "here's to her health!"

A deep silence fell so that everyone could detect the thought of the Bodhisattva. Avalokiteshvara was now speaking for himself.

"Yes, that is all true. She is sincere with others and with herself. And she possesses the thirty-two required qualities, just as the Shakya clan shows the sixty-four signs of perfection. . . . Furthermore, although they don't know it, King Suddhodano and Queen Maya Devi have been husband and wife several times in the last five hundred years. They were even my parents in one of my earlier lives."

Whereupon the gods said nothing more. An immense light, cascading from the higher heaven of the five Shining Ones, enveloped them. Five colors played brilliantly over them and blended, finally, to signify agreement among the

Dhyani Buddhas. Soon the white reddened, the yellow grew orange, the green and the blue shifted tones; Amitabha glowed a deepening purple, which his splendid reflection Amitayus caught and caused to flash and sparkle on the facets of his thirteen jewels. The great decision had been taken.

II

AND WHAT, MEANWHILE, WERE MEN DOING FAR BELOW ON
their earthly planet?

As always in India, they were toiling, without joy or
zest—but also without despair. For thousands of years men
had struggled to cope with the climate and a chronic dearth
of food. They manifested the passive, stubborn energy of the
plant that is perpetually trodden underfoot. It is a fact that
nothing in the peninsula has ever favored man, neither the
sun, nor the rain, nor the soil. The heat weakens his body and
saps his energy. The monsoon, which should come as a bless-
ing to put an end to the annual powdery drought, bursts over
the earth with a brutality that swells the rivers, erodes the

35

arable lands, and swamps the fields. As for the soil, its surface has been scratched and scratched again, year after year, century after century, until the minerals needed to nourish the crops have retreated far below the exhausted top layers; to dig to a still fertile depth is beyond the toiler's enfeebled strength, beyond his long-since-wearied courage.

He shows no trace of the tenacious drive to work that has been the strength of the Chinese, nor any of their constructive patience that withstands all natural calamities and all ravages of war. Has Nature in India been stingy? Very well, man has adapted himself to indolent enjoyment of that little. Want itself became, with time, a kind of calm satiety.

Of course, in certain areas the soil has been rich and fertile ever since the world began, but here the tree has taken possession of the land and fiercely disputed the plow at every furrow. Even the most resolute ax has faltered before the close-serried trunks, the thick underbrush, and the densely entangled lianas.

What help could he invoke, man asked himself. To what Powers had he to pray for even a moment's respite? If it was true that the heavens, the sun, the rain, the wind, the earth, could be controlled by man, what words had he to utter, what price had he to pay so that his prayers would be answered? And if prayers were of no avail, if life had to endure eternally burdensome and lusterless, if all hope of comfort or ease on earth was denied, did there exist, perhaps, "somewhere in the beyond" a haven of grace where he might finally rest in blessedness?

These questions aroused deep anxiety in the people of ancient India, and engendered other no less troubling puzzles: What is this mysterious inner self that quickens the mind, the eye, and the hand, that incites a man to dance at weddings and to weep for those who have gone? Does it return to the earth with the body? Does it, by any happy chance, live on? If so, does it remain near the living who have known it, and cherished or hated it? Does it preserve some memory of wrongs it has suffered and seek to avenge them? Or does some new state of blessedness bring oblivion?

If a state of beatitude exists, how can man attain it? Is it within reach of all, without distinction?

Surely not. An evil man, a thief, a murderer cannot enjoy the same peaceful fate as the person whose passing everyone mourns—the faithful and fertile wife, the affectionate father, the just and upright leader, the obedient subject. Indeed, when the loincloth of the slave and the gold-threaded robes of the king have slipped to the ground, is it possible that the breath animating serf and sovereign will be weighed on the same scales? Will their leavening good actions and honest thoughts be balanced against the leaden burden of their evil acts and impure desires?

It was in terms of questions such as these that the Indian first conceived of his gods, first surmised that he had a soul, and pondered on its destiny. As the centuries rolled on, ideas multiplied and developed. Simple men found in them a ray of sunshine that not only magnified their earthly misery but somehow also justified it until it became necessary to them. Other men could find no satisfaction in answers that posed, in turn, new and subtle questions, and these men foundered in agonizing confusion. Others were crushed by the concept of a spiraling transcendency that led them to consider the body an obstacle to the intuitive vision of hidden things; they constructed dizzying philosophical scaffolds that had no foundation in any logic. Still others conceived of a great Unity, yet they perceived this unity only in the explosion of minute particles—of men, animals, plants, of all that exists, visible or invisible.

And, lastly, there were some who undertook to help and enlighten their fellow men, to speak in their behalf the words that appease the Powers that be, and to guide them toward a happy afterlife. These men were descendants of the Aryans who had come down into India from the north, from Persia and even much farther away. In a slow inundation that lasted a thousand years and more, these strangers had first occupied the Indus plain and then the whole of north India; by virtue of their light skin and their pose as "free and noble" men, they promptly assigned unto themselves the right to lead the hapless human flocks that the Indian sky and soil had so cruelly weakened.

It took many centuries for men to progress from the materially primitive existence of the earliest times to the elaboration of highly abstract cosmic philosophies, and, finally, an understanding of the lofty morality that the Buddha was to preach. Throughout these long years, Indians eddied about in a whirl of beliefs that became less and less comprehensible as they grew more and more complex. Even those who were responsible for acting as interpreters between mankind and the gods often lost their footing; they were sometimes obliged to create new gods to help explain the inexplicable.

So it happened that ten, twenty, fifty times, divine usurpers dispossessed divine incumbents and promoted themselves to first place in heaven, and men were forced to accept one hierarchy after another. The Olympus of India has always been so—a dense tropical forest in which the trees steal the light of life from each other.

Avalokiteshvara's descent to earth upset man's notion of the celestial order once more. When the Bodhisattva chose the woman from whose body his earthly reflection would be born (she having already been, in five hundred instances in her anterior existences, the mother of such a predestined one), the people of India knew nothing whatever about the Tushita heaven, for example, or the five Jinas, or the seven levels of paradise. It took them many decades after the earthly disappearance of the Buddha to become familiar with these new divine wonders.

Even then, the earlier elements of faith did not disappear; over some six thousand years, an edifice of superimposed beliefs, disparate and contradictory—rather like a thick-walled temple fashioned from the materials of previous buildings—sprang up around the heart and mind of India. Luckily, the men of the peninsula have always proved to be masters in the art of reconciling the irreconcilable. As we seek our way through the veritable jungle of Indian thought, we may fail to find pathways that only they are able to follow. Yet the proliferation of ideas and what seem to us the contradictions may be only tokens of their inventiveness in constructing a monument of prodigious unity; if this is the case, then they, as builders, have achieved a deeply impressive continuity.

When a storyteller in India or Tibet starts to relate the history of the Perfect One, his listeners see him gesture, suddenly, in discouragement. He has just realized how impossible it is to go on without explaining what happened "before." He will break off, and for a long time he—and his listeners—will sit in silence. He will allow the Bodhisattva to announce his great news to the Thirty-three and then, with almost heroic zest, he will leap back into ages past, back to the source of it all.

Once upon a time, some three billion four hundred and twenty million years ago, the creative Breath thickened into a vapor that assumed the human form of a giant. This was Divinity itself, unconscious, uncreated, without past or future, and quite beyond human conception. From its belly a cow emerged, fashioned of dense smoke; this was Aditi, the universal Mother. Despite the fact that this cosmic, nourishing goddess later fell from her high estate—even her name was forgotten—it is in her honor that, from the Himalayas to Cape Comorin, the cow has remained the one animal sacred above all others.

By her mooing, Aditi—"the Mother without Father," as she was called—aided the Sky and the Earth to come into being in their turn. Then, again through her help, the eight planets—the Non-Connected, the Immortals—were born, one of which, Surya the Shining One, or the Sun, did not go, like his brothers, to hide in the shades of Earth; he remained in the sky to give life to our globe.

In his turn, the Sun loosed his arrows against the giant. He thus delivered from it Cloud, who became his bride, his daughter Ushas, or the rosy Dawn, the Moon, the Night, and his sons, the bright, handsome Asvins, and many, many others. Like Rudra, for example, the god of thunder; Agni the Consumer, who lives in fire; the quick-tempered, heroic Indra; and Brahma, whose breath animates all that lives.

One, two, perhaps three billion years were consecrated to this series of births. Brahma brought it to a close. Rather ungratefully, he decided that the work of Aditi was finished and he despatched the sacred cow to pasture in the very highest heaven.

Once this splendid creation, which we have described all too briefly, was completed, word of it traveled down to earth, arriving here hundreds of millions of years later. The Indian world had already emerged from primeval clay: the human intellect functioned; spiritual motives now helped to guide man's practical actions that assure his survival. Even desire, which is the germ of mind, had been born. Aryan invaders and natives alike glimpsed the dawn of a brighter future. In their intoxication with the marvelous, Indians accepted unflinchingly the dizzying blood ties that united the great gods. Such and such a powerful one was at once his own

father, wife, and children; another answered to several names
—indeed, several different gods bore the same name. People
also learned not to be greatly astonished by changes in the
celestial hierarchy. Varuna, for example, had established the
universal and immutable order of things; he acted as the
guardian of legality and of magic mysteries; he held the power
to punish evildoers and to forgive the repentant. Yet one day
Varuna found himself relegated to the modest role of gov-
ernor of the waters of heaven and earth.

Of all these willful gods, born of man's agonized dismay
when confronted by the forces of Nature—born, also, of his
efforts to explain the creation and organization of the world—
no trace remains for us today except the prayers men offered
to implore divine mercy. There are no formal likenesses. In
those remote times, the Indian felt no need to fashion any
image of his gods; they were too intimate a part of himself.
For that matter, he thought his gods had passions similar to
his own but enlarged on a celestial scale. This, he reasoned,
was why the gods could listen sympathetically to his prayers,
and it came as no surprise to him that in heaven as on earth, in-
gratitude, jealousy, and competitiveness reigned.

Communication between a man and his gods was not
direct, however. As we have said, certain Aryans undertook
to find the right words and to sing the right hymns to mollify
or to move the heavenly powers, and to perform various rites
in their honor. These priests refused to record their formulas
so that others could use them, and insisted that it was their
prerogative to address the gods. In this way, the caste of the
Brahmans came into being, so called because these men were
custodians of the Brahman, or holy prayer. Later, about 1500
B.C., the Brahmans did undertake the vast job of recording
and editing their knowledge in the sixty books of the Vedas,
or Sacred Texts. The Sanskrit word *"veda"* also means
"heard," which is appropriate for this material that was trans-

mitted orally for so long thanks to the highly disciplined memories of generations of priests.

Presently, the Brahmans were not content simply to be the spokesmen for mankind before the gods. The myth of Purusha gave them a new idea. Purusha was thought of as a primeval man who existed long before the universe was founded. The gods, presumably, were his children. They sacrificed him, and from his divine body the universe was created. Inspired by this myth, the Brahmans established a ritual of sacrifice—of animals, certainly, and perhaps even of prisoners of war and of virgins. Initially, the sacrifice was to propitiate the gods and to win their help. Then the theory was evolved that the gods depended on sacrifice, that they yearned for it because it gave them life. This meant that the Brahmans virtually held the survival of the gods in their hands. Far from merely imploring indulgence, they could very nearly barter: "I give so much, you give so much."

These public sacrifices must have been impressive spectacles. The Chief Brahman, who knew all the holy texts by heart, supervised a prayer leader, who recited hymns from the Rig-Veda: he marked time for the chanting of the cantilenas from the Sama-Veda; he did not miss one syllable of the liturgical formulas in the Yajur-Veda, which the sacrificer repeated as he performed the rituals. If one word was skipped, one movement imperfectly performed, one tiny detail of the liturgy neglected, the sacrifice was ruined and everything had to be done again from the beginning.

Naturally, the altar fire and the libation, which were the dominant elements in the ritual, were deified in time. They eventually supplanted the gods they had helped to keep alive. Agni—the Flesh-Eater, Fire, god of the hearth and friend to man, indispensable mediator between earth and heaven, glowing source of life, Lord of Wisdom, devouring Purity— was honored above Surya the Sun, Varuna, Rudra, and even

Brahma. Next to Agni, Soma, the elixir of immortality extracted from a mysterious plant (probably an alcoholic liquid that fed the altar fire), was reverenced for creating light and, like the sun, infusing the spark of life.

Man had come far, indeed. From passively enduring the yoke of Nature, he had reached a point where he was refashioning it in fantasy. Once set in motion, the Indian mind could not stop. It discovered secondary gods and lesser divinities, both friendly and hostile. While these figures became increasingly metaphysical in concept, they also were strongly animistic. Naturally enough, the poisonous flowers of black magic also sprang up in this divine jungle. And all these beliefs and observances were brought and kept under the control of the priests.

The Brahmans were not an organized clergy; they operated individually, functioning within a family group. Every Brahamn knew the Vedas, in which magnificent hymns alternate with nonsense rhymes, and tips on dice-playing follow subtle philosophical dissertations. He knew how to reconcile the conflicting beliefs that time had sedimented in these books of Knowledge. With the Atharva-Veda and its miscellany of prayers, charms, hymns, and spells etched in his memory, the Brahman officiated in the home, presiding over the traditional ceremonies that accompanied birth, marriage, and death. He caused the rain to fall; he exorcised evil spirits. If he was the deus ex machina of man's daily life, he also kept track of the slow revolutions in Olympus, and even helped out there a bit.

This privileged caste sensed that the sovereignty of the gods had long since been undermined. (It had been threatened ever since the day when, in a fit of boredom, they had fashioned a beautiful little plaything for themselves and called him Manu, the first man.) Attentively, the Brahmans followed the evolution of men's minds toward ever greater refinement, and they were prepared, therefore, when the time came, to effect a smooth transition, without one false step, from the archaic pantheon to a new divine empire. The decline of the earlier gods disturbed them not a whit; for chief deity in the new hierarchy they gave their support to Vishnu, a minute godling who heretofore had been quite insignificant. And so it happened that the Dwarf God arose to take man under his protection; before long he was revealing to man that he had a soul; man's chief concern, he declared, via the Brahmans, should be to safeguard this soul.

The notion that it might be possible to win salvation genrated new questions and beliefs to haunt minds already over-inclined to complications. The origin of life was again uncertain. The holy books put it this way: "As the thread issues from the spider and the tree from the seed, as fire springs from stick rubbed against stick, so was the universe formed from the substance of Brahma." But how frustrated the god must feel who cannot be sure where he himself comes from. Behind Brahma there seemed to loom a shadowy *true* divinity, of which he was only the creative emanation.

Soon very few of the old heavenly company were left. Rudra was transformed into Siva. Indra survived, probably because he was more hero than god. Saturated with soma—until one could have said of him, as of the king of Poland, that when he drank heaven got drunk—he was passionate, strong as a giant, hot-tempered, full of the joy of life. Once he had killed Vita, a dragon that was threatening the Indian Olympus, and had recovered his colleagues' herds of cattle. On another occasion, assisted by Vayu, god of the winds, and by the Maruts, who drew Rudra's chariot, he had gone in search of rain to put an end to the drought. Who would dare do away with this prince of fertility, whom the entire peninsula adored? Furthermore, he deserved to be honored by all those who carry a weapon because he had helped the Aryans subdue the dark-skinned Dravidians. So Indra the Violent One survived to find a place in the story of the Buddha, although, in one sense, he is the very last person one would expect to find there.

Under this new regime, the men of India looked to Ushas the Dawn not to worship her but only to discover what kind of weather she was bringing. They blessed the rain that put an end to the drought, but were as quick to curse it when it swelled the rivers dangerously. The sun was not thanked for having ripened the wheat; fire had no function other than to cook food and keep bodies warm during the cold nights.

To the new religion philosophers and theologians gave a cosmic character that satisfied the very human aspiration to return to the mystery of the origin of things and to discover their first cause, to surprise at his work Him who creates, preserves, destroys, and recreates all life. A concept of monotheism was born that overshadowed the pantheon of gods, scintillating as they were. Deep in his heart, man was not mistaken: the multiplicity of divine figures and names and attributes was only an embroidering on a great veil that, if ever it was raised, must reveal one supreme Master.

Yet the ritual gesture had still to be made, the sacred word had still to be pronounced. The Brahmans were more indispensable than ever, and more truly powerful than any temporal ruler. The people's submissiveness had none of the despair born of a crushed revolt, for rebellion was impossible. If men are to rise against firmly entrenched authority, they must first recognize and accept the idea of individuality and value the feelings, thoughts, and rights of individuals. The Indian of that day had no thoughts or feelings other than those that the public mind and collective acceptance impressed on him. King Suddhodano, in whose family the Buddha had decided to be born again, certainly never had trouble with unruly subjects. Men no more dreamed of throwing off the yoke of royal rule than they did of rejecting a world order divinely established. All their will, it seemed, was devoted to renouncing the world; speculation prevailed over action. The caste system was decreed by a law that was beyond challenge; it had delivered men over to powers solidly established now and forever.

Innately superior to the run of mankind, the Brahmans were also endowed with magic powers, and only they could open or close a pathway to heaven. If they now spoke of the soul's possible salvation through transmigration (on which point all were by no means in agreement), they had, on the other hand, added to the submissiveness of Indian life the fear of pollution. This devouring anxiety loomed over men day and night; it cast its shadow over conscience, speech, and action; it affected not only men's attitudes toward their own bodies but penetrated even to the innermost recesses of their spirit. The Brahmanic jungle, more entangling than ever, enveloped the kingdom of the heart entirely.

Men suffered and persevered on their harsh earth, just as they had six thousand years earlier. They did not know, any more than did the Brahmans, that their gods were already bending the knee before a light that would eventually dominate them. Baffled by theories and speculations beyond their grasp, manipulated by powers beyond their control, they simply waited, yearning dimly for some thunderbolt from heaven to bring them hope, love, and some proof that their life had meaning.

III

FOR CENTURIES THE PRINCIPALITY OF THE SHAKYAS HAD BEEN governed by the Gautamas. It was an old and illustrious family, which traced its descent from the famous hero Ikshvahu, no less. Such prestige allowed Suddhodano to call himself, as his ancestors had before him, Prince of the Shakyas.

If ever there was a fortunate country, this was one. It nestled in the valley where, thanks to Siva, the sacred waters of the Ganges flowed gently across the plain, mirroring the flight of clouds rather than ravaging the fields with torrential floods. When the peasants raised their heads and looked to the north, they saw the snow-clad barrier of the Himalayas, the white crests of the mountains of Nepal, and a hundred

47

glittering peaks around which the monsoon draped shifting gray scarves heavy with fructifying rains.

Prince Suddhodano had already ascended the throne and was reigning from his capital city, Kapilavastu, when the gods of India held their conference in heaven to hear the Bodhisattva. He was a great feudal landowner and drew his wealth from the rice crop. While he, in turn, was actually a vassal of the king of Kosala, he was so wise, so steady of purpose, and so revered by his subjects that his overlord had gladly consented to his taking the title of king.

His wife Maya Devi was no less accomplished. Suddhodano's father had specified such superlative qualities in his future daughter-in-law that the young girl his envoys had finally singled out for his approval was surely unique in the whole peninsula. She was so breath-takingly beautiful that it was hard to believe such perfection could exist on this earth; her parents, companions, and even her husband smilingly called her Maya, which means "illusion." She enchanted more than the eyes; her voice was as melodious as a harp, and her conversation beguiled the minds of her listeners and filled their hearts with inexpressible sweetness.

She also honored the gods. Indeed, she was so devout that if ever a cloud passed over the royal couple her piety was the cause. The Queen searched so intensely for a spiritual absolute that she denied the pleasures of the body. She did not dance; she was mindful in disrobing never to admire the exquisite lines of her thighs; for food she contented herself with a bit of fruit; and—so it is said—she had refused to share her lord's bed, although she loved him more than any living creature.

King Suddhodano desired his wife passionately, but he loved her so deeply that he refused to insist on his rights and respected the wishes of this companion who was so avid for perfect purity. He took care to meet her only in public, for he feared that she might give in to his desire and thus lose all she had achieved to draw nearer the gods. He watched her as she passed on her way to the altars, her arms laden with flowers; he listened to the admiring murmur that followed her at every step, and he retired alone to a bed in which he found no joy. For Maha Prajapati, sister of Maya, tender and loving as she was, could not satisfy his heart.

The intimacy—or absence of it—in the relationship between Maya Devi and her husband has been argued for centuries, all the more heatedly because the experts never really know what goes on in a bedroom, even a royal one. On the other hand, the people of India, in the simplicity of their hearts, have shown a consistent preference for the Buddha's sire to be a white elephant with six fine ivory tusks. We will abide by this.

Twelve years passed from the day when the Bodhisattva informed the gods of his decision. Then, in the summer of 545 B.C., a series of signs began to appear in the chaste household of King Suddhodano, in Kapilavastu, and even in the surrounding countryside. Gardens were suddenly free of weeds and thistles, roads were clear of dust, rooms in the palace were empty of all those biting, sucking, buzzing insects that seem to have been created only to try men's patience. Even the tiny water serpents vanished from the pools. Presently, wild birds came from the forest to perch like familiars on the palace balustrades and accept seeds offered by the astonished ladies of the court. In the streets, the meandering cows gave proof of rare discretion and, stationing themselves before the fruit stalls, waited tranquilly for the merchant himself to come fetch them cinnamon apples and mangoes. Soon a third sign was seen: trees simultaneously put forth blossoms, leaves, and fruit.

Miracle followed upon miracle at such a pace that there

was no time left to marvel. They became particularly numerous and unusal as one drew near the palace. In the garden pools, lotuses as large as chariot wheels blossomed and did not fade; lice abandoned the roses; slugs deserted the flower beds; moles forebore digging up the turf of the lawns. The stores of butter, oil, and honey, which usually were prodigally wasted, seemed not to grow less. The same was true of the coffers which held the treasure amassed by the King's ancestors: the gold coins, pearls, rubies, and silver jewelry, which the young sovereigns were in the habit of distributing liberally to the poor (who never quite knew what to do with such gifts and took them to the moneylenders), seemed never to diminish. And one day the musical instruments sounded, although no one had touched them, and, at twilight, a supernatural glow chased the shadows from the royal chambers.

The rays of the July sun were sifting through a light morning haze when Queen Maya Devi came to tell her husband about her dream—a delicious dream but a very strange one.

"Imagine, my lord, that what I am about to tell you began in my own apartments here in the palace. Four kings came into my bedchamber without knocking. For some reason, I did not feel frightened. They did not speak, they simply bowed to me; then they took my couch by the four corners and lifted it into the air. I felt as if I were floating on a pillow of clouds. . . . They set me down on a mountain peak. It was in the Himalayas, and I thought I recognized it as Nanda Devi. But this is the curious thing: there was a tree planted on the very summit of the mountain."

"Very curious! Who has ever heard tell of so much as a tuft of lichen growing among the eternal snows."

"A green tree, my lord . . . Then three queens presented themselves. They were carrying a chest, and they took a gold sari from it, and a green blouse, and . . . well, then they dressed me. And they combed my hair. . . . Finally, they led me into a palace with walls like transparent gold. From the windows I could look out on a landscape such as is not to be found within a hundred leagues in your kingdom."

The King was following her account with keen attention.

"Hush! Listen! That is nothing. . . . A young elephant came into the room. He was as white as mountain snow and as bright as the moon. He was this big. . . . You won't believe it! He had a flesh-colored head and six splendid ivory tusks! Six! And on the tip of his trunk he was carrying a lotus. He kneeled and offered me the flower. Then he came near me and gently, ever so gently, sank one of his tusks in my side. But he didn't hurt me at all. . . . After that . . . After that, I don't know. . . . A bluebird woke me up, I think. . . . Isn't it a marvelous dream? I have the most wonderful feeling just from telling you about it. . . . But you look upset?"

"No. No. I was just thinking that we must have this dream explained to us," the King replied.

As was the custom, Suddhodano called together the wise men who were most renowned in the interpretation of dreams. They were three old, old Brahmans who, once the Queen had been dismissed by a tender glance from her husband, consulted together with all the gravity doctors affect at the bedside of an invalid. Then, after a period of reflection that lasted till evening, the one who seemed to be as old as the banyan tree of the pagoda of Siva began to speak.

"There is no doubt, Sire, that this is a great dream of annunciation. Do not be disturbed; it is a happy dream. Your wife will give birth to a son."

"Ah, a son of my own! . . . What happiness!"

"I said, your wife will give birth to a son. A bodhisattva

has already entered her, through her side, and he will appear on earth in the form of a newborn infant, whom our Queen will bring into the world in ten months. This son will reign over no earthly kingdom but over the souls of men. If he ascends the throne, he will be the greatest monarch in the universe; he will conquer by the love he bears all men and not by arms. Ah! wait one moment. . . . I think rather that he will leave his own hearth and will renounce the world. . . . Yes . . . yes, and he will succeed in tearing away the veil of ignorance that shrouds the earth. He will be called the Enlightened One, the Buddha. . . . Oh, Sire, the day of deliverance is near! The son whom the Queen carries in her womb will be the glorious sun of truth. Let us all rejoice!"

Nothing remained but for the three Brahmans to go prostrate themselves before Maya Devi. A moment later, the ruler of the Shakyas also entered her chamber and bowed low before her. He was a perplexed, anxious, immensely proud king—and a slightly downcast husband.

The months rolled by. Spring came and passed. When May appeared, with her retinue of birds and flowers, the Queen's time had come. One morning, Maya Devi stepped into a chariot that bore her to the summer residence King Suddhodano had had built in Lumbini, some seven or eight leagues from the capital. The Queen was as slender as ever and nothing suggested a forthcoming happy event. But if humans could be misled, the gods knew. Above the imposing train of ladies in waiting and servants who accompanied the maharani, another train floated, invisible, in the sky—the bright divinities of the paradise of the Thirty-three. Gandharvas, singers, and musicians, and thousands of Apsarases swept along in a kind of intoxicated, cradling dance. All seven hundred eighty billion gods had been alerted.

In Lumbini, wandering from grove to copse, the Queen

paused at the foot of a tall tree that stood as erect as the pillar of a temple and that was covered with shining foliage and fragrant buds. She felt no pain, indeed not even any discomfort, but she sensed that the sacred moment was at hand. As her companions discreetly withdrew, whispering among themselves, the tree bent over Maya and enclosed her in a cradle of tender leaves. A few seconds later, the bare ground was suddenly blanketed with a thick green sward over which thousands and tens of thousands of flowers were scattered like a rug far more beautiful than any a Kashmiri craftsman had ever dreamed of. From a nearby rock a crystal spring gushed forth.

No one was present at the birth except Brahma, who parted the curtaining clouds to peer down from heaven, and Indra, who was disguised as an old woman so as not to offend the modesty of the young mother. Posterity would have known nothing about it, if the Queen had not related the miracle later. It seems that, rousing herself from a drowsiness that had suddenly overcome her, she had discovered a tiny infant lying next to her; without hurting her, it had emerged from her side where the elephant of her dream had pierced her. The infant was lying on an immense white lotus.

Beneath the little boy—the child's sex was the first thing the mother made sure of—stretched a net of gold. Four Apsarases grasped the corners of the net and dipped its burden in the spring. The Guardians of the World, the five Jinas, cast their sparkling, bejeweled reflections over its crystalline water to begin the purification ceremony. The kings of the Nagas, Nanda and Upananda, half-emerging from a cloud, sprayed streams of warm and cool water over the child's hands. Then, as drops of scented water and fragrant petals sifted down, two archangels descended from the skies, one bearing a parasol, the other a fan made from the tail of a yak.

Emerging from the crystal-clear water, the infant bounded from the net and looked about him. Majestic as a small lion, he paced seven steps toward the north, then seven each toward the other cardinal points. Wonder-struck, the Queen watched and listened as he took possession of the world. In each footprint of the prodigious, naked little man, still moist from his first bath, white lotuses sprang up. His words were scarcely less amazing than his behavior.

"I walk in first place in the world. . . . This is my final birth. I will put an end to the sorrow which birth, illness, old age, and death bring!" he cried joyously. "In the midst of all beings, I will be without superior."

He leaned over and pointed toward the earth.

"I will conquer the demon in behalf of those plunged in the fires of hell. I will make fall the healing rain which is security under the law, so that all men will be filled with joy and well-being. . . ."

And, raising his head to heaven, he declared himself master of space: "I will look above all beings."

Thus, in word and thought, the master of memory and all knowledge, the saviour of the world, soared to the peak of the universe; he had crossed the seven cosmic spheres where the seven planets revolve; he had abolished time and space.

Having spoken, the marvelous little creature became like any other newborn infant. The tree parted, making way for the servants, who were devoured by curiosity. The radiant mother and her child were borne off on a litter. But concealed under the garb and humble appearance of porters, the Guardians of the World, who had come down from Mount Meru, were actually supporting the shafts: the Angel of the East, dressed in silver, bore a shield studded with pearls; the Angel of the South, armed with a shield of sapphires, was riding a blue horse; the Angel of the North glittered with gold; the

Angel of the West, carrying a coral shield, bestrode his three ruby-red steeds. No human eye, however, perceived any of this magnificence.

Like any ordinary mother, Maya was watching her son in tender amazement. Tentatively she touched the strange signs that marked the little body and tirelessly she measured and remeasured the extraordinary length of his ears.

"They are very long, it is true," she murmured. "My own little elephant."

Book Two

I

IT WAS LEARNED, LATER, THAT AT THE PRECISE MOMENT THE child of Queen Maya was born—and, naturally, no one but the three wise men questioned his being also the son of King Suddhodano—the blind had recovered their sight and the deaf their hearing, while sanity and memory were restored to the mad. The King was impressed, but, prudent as always, he wished to be sure that so much good fortune was not a prelude to terrible catastrophes. Thus does the secretly discontented heart doubt the most propitious signs.

"Your son," the soothsayers announced, with due solemnity and flourish, "is one of those sovereign princes, one of whom is born every thousand years to govern the whole world. Already he possesses, in full potency, the seven treasures, which you will recognize presently."

"Seven treasures! For me there is only one, and that is—"

"Seven! The Golden Disk of Vishnu, which with his right hand he will roll into all the regions over which he will be master. And the Crown of Pearls, whose soft radiance lights the quarters of the women so that, in the dark of night, it seems that the sun is shining. Then there is Aswa, the blue-coated horse, tireless and forever young, on which he will gallop through the clouds; Hasti, the elephant white as snow, whose supernatural strength will carry him wherever he wishes. And there is the astute Minister; the invincible General; and, rarest of all jewels, Istri Ratna, woman of incomparable grace, more radiant than the dawn. Ah, your son will be a true Shakravartin, a Sovereign of the Wheel, a Master of the World!"

Reassured albeit also amazed, the King lifted the infant on his knees and pressed him against his chest, and with this gesture consecrated him as the successor to continue his royal line. Then, bethinking himself that he must take his young heir to the temple and present him to the gods, he gave orders that the streets should be swept and sprayed with attar of roses, the trees decorated with lanterns and torches, and the populace dressed in holiday attire. There was great revelry throughout the city. The crowds pressed close to watch clowns, jugglers, snake charmers, rope dancers, and dancing girls in spangled robes with bells tinkling around their ankles. Mummers dressed in skins of bear or antelope danced on street corners, animal tamers put their tigers through their paces, athletes competed, trainers loosed their fighting quail for the people to bet on. The air vibrated with the rumble of drums, the strident voices of oboes, the whispering of flutes, and the throaty insistence of plucked brass strings.

The crowd was so dense that, although the guards shouldered people back, one procession could not get near the palace. Word had spread quickly through the provinces that the most handsome prince in the world had been born, and the feudal lords were competing to be first to offer gifts of good omen to the parents. Four great kings of central India met that day on the royal square, and history has handed their names down to us: Pradyota, King of Ujjayini; Udayana, of Kuchambi; Bimbisara, King of Magadha, who was later to become a faithful friend of the Perfect One; and, lastly, Prasenajit of Kosala, liege lord of the Shakyas. Golden platters carried high above the bearers' heads were heaped with precious rarities: shawls woven of kid's hair, so fine that they could be slipped through a child's ring; fragrant spikenard; turquoise the color of the evening sky; pearl-studded belts; caskets of sandalwood; mammoth grains of rice and chick-peas; fabrics so transparent that, folded a dozen times, they would not veil a virgin's face.

The rejoicing was not limited to Kapilavastu. From one end of the kingdom to the other, money flowed from purse to counter until prosperity made faces bloom and rounded the bellies of merchants and peasants alike. Nothing that was for sale was left unbought—rich gifts for the happy royal couple, festive garments, flowers, jewels—not to mention all that was eaten, too, since happiness makes for a good appetite. And so the populace called the little boy Sarvarthasiddha—"He who brings prosperity." But simple people have the habit of shortening proper names, and this was soon changed to Siddhartha, an elision that crossed the threshold of the palace gates and was delightedly adopted by King Suddhodano, because it means "He who has achieved his goal."

Daily cares were forgotten as everyone, from the humblest Sudra to warriors proud of their noble rank, joined in the celebration. There was also a surprise. Although the ceremony at the temple was held in secret, as is proper when a newborn infant of royal birth is presented to the gods, a rumor flashed through the city that the divine ones had actually appeared and kneeled before the child. Some versions even claimed that they had sung a hymn in his honor.

> *Mount Meru, the Monarch of the World, the Axis of the*
> *World has not to bow before the mustard seed.*
> *The Ocean could not bow before the water caught in*
> *the print of the cow's hoof.*
> *Neither Moon nor Sun could bow before a firefly.*
> *And how could He who possesses Wisdom bow before the*
> *gods?*
> *Therefore do we kneel before Thee.*

Among the strangers arriving in Kapilavastu was a hermit who presented himself before the King. He was a rishi, a meditating monk emaciated by fasting, who had come down directly from the Himalayas. His skin had been darkened by the bite of the elements, and the herald, not knowing his name, announced him simply as Asita—the "Black One."

He was a man of so venerable an air that Maya, sensing that he *knew*, bowed low before him, lifted the infant from her breast and laid the child at the old man's feet.

"Ah! Do not do that, Lady!" And the rishi bowed eight times, touching his forehead to the ground so that his bald skull was lower than the stiffly curving little legs. He murmured ecstatically, "I did understand what the devas whispered to me in my meditations." Then he stood upright and, palm to palm, he added: "Holy child! I worship thee. Thou art He! I see in thee the rosy-tinted light, the lines on the soles of the feet, the faint mark of the swastika, the thirty-two principal sacred signs, and the eight marks of lesser import. Thou art the Enlightened One. Thou wilt preach the Law, and for thousands upon thousands upon thousands of years all men who learn thy rules will be saved."

The King of the Shakyas was listening pensively to the exalted ascetic.

"Know, O King, that a heavenly lotus has sprung from thy royal house. I dare not say thy happy house, for thy very bowels will be torn because of this child. I do not worship Brahma in this creature, but the child himself. The child himself! He will open wide the heavy gates of despair, he will free men from the toils of ignorance, he will deliver the poor, the miserable, and the hopeless from their bondage."

Tears were flowing down the deep lines of his face and were lost in his unkempt white beard.

"You see me weep," the ascetic added bitterly, "because I shall die before this child becomes the Illumined One. I will not hear the words of the Master unfurl the cloud of compassion over the heads of suffering mankind and quench the fires of its pain."

Sadly he turned toward the Queen.

"Gentle Mother, thou art dear to gods and to men for this birth; thou hast become too holy to suffer longer. . . ."

The assembled nobles had withdrawn, dismissed by a gesture from the King and, in the corridors of the palace, were busily trying to interpret the words of Asita. The King was questioning the hermit in private. He knew, by hearsay, that rishis who have grown deaf to the sounds of the world have mastered, in their retreat, the five transcendental sciences. Beyond doubt, in his rapture this man would have seen—if one may call it seeing—marvelous things, and would have heard strange words inaudible to profane ears.

"A little while ago you spoke of sacred signs that mark this child as destined for some prodigious undertaking. I see no signs."

"They will appear, they will appear. . . . His skull will develop a protuberance. His hair, plaited on the right side, will be as blue as the throat of a peacock. Low on his smooth, broad forehead a little tuft of silver hair will grow between his eyebrows. His eyes, fringed by lashes as long as those of a young heifer, will be large, black and white. The lobes of his ears will be three times as long as yours. His jaw, as strong as a lion's, will have forty even, solid, and very white teeth, and he will have a long pointed tongue."

The hermit's transported manner made it seem that he was actually "seeing" these strange signs.

"He will have delicate, golden skin, a body as supple and firm as the stalk of an arum, well-rounded thighs, legs like a gazelle's, seven protuberances, and a torso as powerful as a Punjab tiger's. He will hold himself very erect, even when seated. When he is standing with his arms hanging free, they will reach to his knee. The back of his hands will be broad, his palms flat, his nails thick. His very long fingers, as well as his toes, will be joined by a thin membrane."

Stunned, the King did not utter a word.

"The hair of his body will grow one filament at a time, and the hairs on his arms will grow upward. What must be hidden will be drawn up. On the soles of his feet will be traced a wheel with a thousand spokes. His voice will sound exactly like that of Brahma."

Completely overcome, Suddhodano listened silently as the black-skinned Asita undertook to expound to him the eighty secondary signs: invisible veins; nails bowed and copper-red; a voice like the trumpeting of an elephant and yet of penetrating sweetness; scarlet mouth; rounded finger tips; invisible joints; deeply etched and symmetrical lines on the palm. . . .

"Know, O King," said the rishi, in ecstatic conclusion,

"that he will be the flower of our human tree, the flower that
blooms once in thousands of years but that, when full blown,
fills the world with the perfume of Knowledge and the honey
of Love."

Asita had prophesied truly. Seven days after the miraculous birth, Queen Maya Devi fell smilingly into a sleep from
which she did not waken. She had departed for those ethe-
real regions where pain does not exist. The gods could grant
her no greater grace than to spare her the grief she would
have felt to see her son leave her and wander through the
world as a mendicant monk. And then, too, after bearing
the Buddha, her womb would have been too holy to shelter
a child of mortal race. To those who mourned her, the years
she had spent on earth seemed brief, and they wondered if
truly she had not been the goddess Illusion herself and not a
beautiful and matchless Queen whom they had respectfully
cherished.

The nurse selected for the infant was the sister of the departed Queen. In the space of one night, the gentle Maha Prajapati felt her breasts swell and flow with milk as rich as that
of a mountain goat. Thirty-two women took turns in caring
for the child: eight bathed him; eight carried him about; eight
watched over his sleep; eight were ordered to hover smilingly
over the tiny infant so that even if his eyes were still un-
focused, he might sense their tender love.

King Suddhodano could not help but feel beset. All these
miracles and predictions, and the strange tales of the Queen,
tormented him. Not to mention the child himself! A newborn
creature who had walked and talked and then became an ordinary breast-fed infant again! Even now, although he was a
mere child, he had only to appear for every man present to

feel fresh hope spring up in his heart. For three years the
sovereign's perplexity deepened until it almost displaced his
grief for the death of Maya Devi.

He finally decided to seek the advice of the most erudite
Brahman in his principality. A man who was in constant contact with the gods, who had prepared the honey and ghee for
them, who "had acquired understanding"—surely he would
be able to give a valid explanation of such strange things.

A public sacrifice was held with more than usual solemnity. Not one cough or sneeze from the public forced the
officiating priest to stop and repeat from the beginning the
recitation that any untimely disturbance rendered null and
void. Then, in an unbroken contemplative silence, the tongues
of altar fire licked the carcasses of the slaughtered horses,
bearing the love of Earth to its spouse the Heavens. Majesti-
cally, the hymns soared, echoing for men's ears the inaudible
sound that is the voice of inconceivable Primordial Thought.

Afterward, prince and priest sat face to face on the floor,
without ceremony, and looked at each other, allowing long
periods of silence to etch their words on each other's minds.

"Thy spirit and my spirit are as eternal as Brahma the
Absolute. Wert thou to listen to them, thou wouldst hear the
very Word of the Uncreated. They have had no beginning
and they will have no end. But they can act only when clothed
in the envelope of the flesh. Weighed down by it, I should say,
for the body is a burden that brings with it much suffering.
Every man must experience an incalculable succession of existences that are bound together and governed by his karma,
by his deeds and their consequences."

"Yes, this I know. . . ."

"Action and inner subtance, the subtle matter that the
deed creates within the body, have already made thee god or
animal, perhaps, and will make thee plant or man. Karma is
there always, imperishable, clothing itself in a fresh envelope

for each new existence. But, O King, thou canst free thyself of the karma attached to thy spirit and of the need to be reborn. Thou canst be delivered of all that is called 'work' and of all the fruits of action. Deliverance . . ."

The eyes of the King turned from the Brahman toward the door. A child's laugh sounded through the heavy cedar portal. Suddhodano smiled and said absently, "You were saying . . ."

". . . that deliverance lies in the Atman-Brahman, in the Supreme Breath, the Spirit of Life, in Brahman, the Principle of the Universe that is enthroned far, far above and beyond the destinies of this earthly world. He who possesses the Atman becomes insensible to pleasure and to pain. Henceforth he is indifferent to all things, he rises above the sorrows of the heart. He no longer knows father or mother, gods or Vedas, life or death. . . . Then the key word can be spoken: '*Ta tvam asi*,' 'That art thou.' Thou, thy true being, thy spirit is one with the Unity in All. The moment a being knows that he is one with the Infinite, he is delivered of his transient nature and of his rebirths."

The Brahman no longer cared if the King was listening to him. He himself appeared to be soaring upward to melt into the Supreme Breath.

As Suddhodano watched the priest, who sat before him in a motionless transport, he reflected on how greatly religion had changed. The deep concern with salvation, which the Brahman had just voiced, had relegated to second place sacrifice, abstinence, and all the moral duties that the Vedas prescribed as the way to be saved. Now piety was based on knowledge, which alone enabled man to free himself from the chain of rebirth. Asceticism had formerly prepared man for the ritual of sacrifice; now its purpose was to foster the knowledge of salvation and to confer a superhuman, miraculous strength on its practitioners. Suddhodano knew that forests and caves in his kingdom were inhabited by hermits who had retired into solitude to achieve holiness through meditation and self-mortification. He had heard that the sight of these yogis so horrified the gods, who were very conscious of the danger now threatening them, that they dispatched beautiful nymphs to tempt the ascetics and divert them from acquiring too much power. If this were perhaps only rumor, the King knew for a fact that the Brahmans, as a group, were alert to the challenge to their positions as sole arbiters of men's spiritual life. He also knew that his own lay caste, the Kshatriyas, had originated the idea that the mind should free itself, should break away from religious tutelage, and seek salvation independently. At least four Shakya princes before him were known to have abdicated and withdrawn to lonely caves to become holy men.

But despite all this, who could imagine a world so topsy-turvy that a priest should become the pupil of a Kshatriya, as the prophecies about his little son seemed to foretell? The King waited patiently until the Brahman roused from his meditation. The rishi gathered his robe—an immaculate white bordered in red—about his hips and was preparing to leave.

"But . . . I wanted to ask about my son—"

"Thy son?" the priest almost hissed in reply. "Thy son? If he had been of my caste, I would have purified him by giving him the sacred girdle and belt. For years I would have taught him, I would have been at his side to preside over his second birth and to assist him in his first sacrifice. Then I would have celebrated his marriage, purified his son in turn and, before he entered the life of meditation, I would have consecrated my old age to instructing him in the way of salvation."

Disdaining to bow to the King, he moved rapidly toward

the door. He turned back to say curtly, "Let him reign, if he is *thy* son. But if the gods are truly interested in him, they will arrange to put a wise Brahman in his path to guide his stumbling steps."

II

THANKS TO THE CARE OF MAHA PRAJAPATI, WHO HAD BECOME
the first wife of the King of the Shakyas, Siddhartha reached
the age of eight without suffering from too many childhood
diseases, but he was not a particularly robust boy. His solici-
tous father saw to it that he was taught all that a prince should
know. Suddhodano had put the rishi Asita's words out of his
mind. If he ever did fleetingly remember them, he still hoped
that by bringing the boy up as the crown prince he would divert him from the life of suffering and superhuman glory
that had been foretold for him. He entrusted the child to the
care of Vishvamitra, the heir of a famous family of Brahmans
and the most highly regarded teacher in the kingdom.

Seated side by side before a fragrant wood fire, instructor and youthful prince first performed the ritual devotion. Three times Vishvamitra placed a fold of his scarf on the boy's left shoulder, then under his armpit, and holding Siddhartha by the hand, the Brahman made him execute a right circle. In a conversation which Ganesa, god of knowledge, followed attentively, the priest sought to guide the mind and heart of his pupil who, in turn, strove to learn from and to revere the master who deigned to pass on to him his wisdom. At the dialogue's close, the Brahman brushed his hand over the heart and navel of Siddhartha. It was done; the child had experienced a second birth, and had passed into the spiritual life.

As a part of his first lesson, which included his having to look for wood and light the fire, Siddhartha received a book of palm leaves bound between covers of red sandalwood, which were bordered with precious gems. Gripping his reed pen, he listened, with lowered eyes, as the sage slowly dictated, letter by letter, the verse that only those of high birth may hear and that begins with the sacred syllable OM. "OM! Let us meditate on the supreme splendor of the divine Sun. May he illumine our thoughts!" The child pronounced the holy syllable so well, the "o" guttural at first but rising from the throat to the lips, the "m" firmly contained until the whole vibrated like a drum, that the teacher caught his breath.

Then, throwing aside his book, the pupil rapidly traced the miraculous verse in the dust in all twelve Indian alphabets. Certainly he had never learned or even seen them, yet he wrote the letters of all nations, even the symbols used by the inhabitants of the caves, seas, and mountains. And he knew the phonetic accents of the sixty-four languages in which he could write.

"That's enough," said Vishvamitra abruptly. "Let us go on to numbers."

The child counted by twos, tens, hundreds, and thousands. He ended by pointing out without a moment's hesitation how many hairs from the whiskers of a mouse could be placed side by side in a vodjana, which—as everyone knows—corresponds to the length of two thousands lances placed end to end.

"Thou art the master of thy masters," said the sage, and he threw himself down before the boy. "It is thou who art my teacher. I worship thee, sweet Prince, who have come to my school only to show me that thou knowest everything without need of learning it in books and that thou knowest also the art of respect."

Loosening his own sacred girdle, the priest passed it around the child, arranging the three strands over his left shoulder in such a way that they crossed the chest and met over the right hip, under the loincloth.

It is impossible to say whether King Suddhodano evinced any pleasure at having a son intellectually so highly endowed. While India had long since rid itself of any trace of its earlier barbarism, the men of his time who held power needed only the rudiments of a literary education. For the rest, the innately poetic nature of the race and its tendency to philosophize about the relations between gods and men answered all needs —together with the knowledge, orally transmitted, of the duties and rights that every nobleman should respect. Furthermore, were the Brahmans not there to put their knowledge at the service of the Court? The important thing for a young prince, even before the moral instruction he needed if he was to exercise power wisely in the future, was to be trained in mental agility, physical strength, and courage. It was important, also, for him to acquire that personal charm that wins men's hearts far more effectively than the authority of a title or illustrious birth.

By the time Siddhartha was fifteen, no one could surpass him in the strenuous games of youth. In racing, horseback riding, and archery, no one would have even matched the Prince had he not withdrawn from competition when he was on the verge of winning. If he noticed that the horses were weary or sensed his comrades' disappointment at losing, he would pretend that he had to rest. Often, when a doe bounded off or a frightened peacock fled into the underbrush, his arrow never left the taut bowstring, and with genuine joy he would watch the animal escape to safety.

Siddhartha loved nothing so much as to slip off alone to the lotus pools his father had ordered built for his pleasure. In these shady gardens where the sun's rays were filtered, fresh and cool, through leafy boughs, and by the banks of brooks that slipped softly, like blindworms, through the green sward, he would study the skill of ants, the flight of birds, the miracle of a mauve bud transformed into a radiant white flower.

He had heard of disappointment, pain, and death, but to him these were words he understood only in an abstract way. They were words that referred to things grownups ordinarily prefer to ignore—or to pass over in silence. They were empty words, and he never suspected that, one day, he too would learn their tragic meaning.

The first blood he saw flow, the first spasm of pain he felt under his fingers, he owed to a wounded swan that his cousin Devadatta's arrow had brought down. Siddhartha dressed the wound with honey and fresh leaves, gently smoothed the ruffled feathers, and stroked the wild bird with a hand as light as the young leaf of the banana tree until he had quieted its thudding heart.

The groom who came to claim the prey in his master's name Siddhartha dismissed in a tone of voice that admitted of no reply. "No! If the bird were dead, it would be right to send it to the hunter. But the swan is alive. My cousin has killed only the divine speed that moved this white wing."

The incident created such bad blood between the two cousins that it was brought before the council of ministers. The discussion was at its height—and indecisive, as always if political considerations are paramount—when a strange priest appeared in the room without any door's having opened to admit him. "If life has value," the newcomer said simply, "he who saves a life has a greater right to possess the living thing than has he who tried to kill it." The King rose to thank the wise man for his advice, but he saw only a hooded serpent gliding over the marble floor toward the window. He stood silent, together with his nobles, as this unknown god slipped away into the gardens.

One day, as Siddhartha and his father were walking across the fields, the King bid the boy admire the rich earth rolling in rounded furrows behind the plow. The oxen were pressing their robust shoulders against the creaking yoke, and young boys followed after, spreading a pale golden shower of seed. All around them stood the smiling forest, alive with nests in the low bushes and birds chattering among the tree tops, with gray squirrels and blue ringdoves flitting from branch to branch. The whole world breathed peace, spring, plenitude.

But, looking beyond what stirred his senses, the young Prince perceived the thorns concealed beneath the rose of life. He observed how the laborer toiled to live, how the flanks of the oxen quivered under the whip, how the plow-shares severed the worm. The lizard snapped up the ant, and the kite devoured both. The shrike pursued the swift that hunted the iris-hued butterfly. Everywhere one creature killed a fellow murderer and was killed in turn; everywhere life fed upon death.

"Is this the happy earth you are showing me? . . . I

would like to stay here alone and think about these things."

Siddhartha sat down, his legs crossed under him, beneath a flowering apple tree, and meditated on the profound evil of life and on its remote origin and a possible remedy. Love for all living things, compassion for their condition, and a passion to help them, plunged the young boy in an ecstasy, his first step along the road to Knowledge. The hours passed, and the sun wheeled toward the western mountains. But although the shadows were shifting, the trunk of the apple tree twisted slowly back upon itself, and the rose-tinted shade never slipped from over the bent head.

The child of a working man who was nearby related these things afterward and thus posterity knows of them. This boy felt the breeze stirred by invisible wings that five spirits fanned to and fro to freshen the air around the meditating one. And he heard a voice that seemed to come from the blossoms of the apple tree.

"Leave the son of the King in peace. So long as the shadow has not lifted from his heart, my shade will not fail to shelter him."

III

SUDDHODANO HAD HAD THREE RESIDENCES BUILT FOR HIS SON. One, of squared timbers paneled in cedar, was warm for the winter months; the second, of veined marble, was fresh and cool in the summers; and the third, of baked brick, was roofed with blue tile. Here it was delightful to while away the spring evenings, listening to the nightingales and breathing the fragrance of the tuberoses. Siddhartha spent enchanted hours there, in jovial companionship, for the blood ran rich and young in his veins. Then, suddenly, he would withdraw to the seclusion of a gardener's hut to sit in the shadows of meditation; the brilliance of his spirit was as darkened as is the silver face of a lake tarnished by passing clouds.

At other times he ventured to the boundaries of the royal park. Here the flowering terraces and carefully tended bosks and lawns gave way abruptly to a riotous jungle. Behind lofty tree trunks and through lianas spiked with wild flowers that resembled bizarre monsters, the Prince glimpsed strange men. Hairy and dirty, they were almost naked, and they shuffled along, staring fixedly before them. The most astonishing thing was that his servants bowed respectfully whenever one of these creatures approached and haughtily extended a hand for food to be placed in it. They explained to him that these men were ascetics, men who gave up a comfortable life on earth to assure themselves a desirable place when the time came for them to die. What peculiar behavior! Certainly the Brahmans, who were teaching him about the gods and the cycle of rebirths, prepared for their future blessedness in a much more elegant way! They were clean—indeed, they were beautifully groomed—and they did not envisage winning rebirth by martyrizing their bodies. What would Siddhartha have thought then, had he met one of the fanatics who slash their flesh, or who sit motionless, wasting away, with one arm upraised and eyes eaten by flies, or who drag a heavy temple chariot by means of a hook embedded in their muscles?

Remembering the prophecies, the King was troubled by the musings of his beloved son. Was Siddhartha already considering some distant quest for who knows what? Could he be thinking of giving up everything that is worth keeping?

"He is thinking of love," one of the King's ministers asserted, "and love will cure him. What does he know of beauty, of a woman's perfumed lips and eyes that make a man forget heaven? Bronze chains cannot halt the thoughts that one single hair of a woman's head holds fast."

Suddhodano objected that the Prince was still innocent. What did he know of voluptuous pleasure? He might very well smile and turn away.

77

"It is a question of trying," the minister replied. "Our young master is now eighteen, and that is an age we all have known. Every man carries within him his own image of Woman, and chooses for his vision whatever face seems to him most fitting. Seek out the loveliest girls of our noble Kshatriya families in Kapilavastu and give a banquet where they can be presented to him. We will watch for him to smile on the girl who pleases him most."

In this ancient beauty contest held before a single judge, all contestants were to receive a prize, which Siddhartha would give them. Everyone supposed that he would hold back the most precious—a necklace of rose pearls—for the girl of his choice. For days there was much to-do about clothes, much primping, and much intrigue among the messengers. And tears aplenty.

The night before the presentation was not long enough for all the bathing, perfuming, brushing and dressing of hair this way and that, for glossing eyelashes with antimony powder, and applying a dot of lacquer between the eyebrows. It seemed that dawn arrived earlier than usual, for not one young woman had had time to paint the nails of more than one foot. Not one, for that matter, was dressed when the long trumpets sounded, and more than one shawl was adjusted only in the chariot en route to the banquet.

If in India today the lowliest fisherwoman possesses a gracious distinction and finesse worthy of a princess, one can imagine what, in the year 529 B.C., this gathering of a hundred and eight young noblewomen must have been. A fairy spectacle of delicate pastel mousselines, embroidered silks from China, silver lamés from Persia, scarves of fabrics as diaphanous as a cloud of incense. And the smooth oval faces, lips that outlined a perfect bow of Krishna, splendid dark eyes in which the joy of self-aware beauty contended with anxiety!

Hands like birds poised for flight, shoulders whose rounded fullness was palpable under the fitted corselets, slender throats enhanced by the heavy chignons caught up low on the neck and secured by a black diamond. Anyone who has not seen an Indian woman walk, her hips swaying slightly, the golden bracelets around her ankles tinkling faintly, her head held high, like a dahlia on its pliant stem, cannot easily imagine the beauty of a woman who walks barefoot, draped in the simple harmonious folds of a sari.

If any young woman felt any confidence at all that morning, it deserted her at sight of the Prince. Whether tender or ardent or smiling, all eyes stared fixedly at the ground as each girl curtsied low before him. Not one of them looked up even when the hand of Siddhartha held out her gift. When the public applauded one or another it found particularly beautiful, she stood for a moment as if stunned, and then fled like a gazelle, startled by the contact with that highborn hand.

To the stupefaction of the Court, the pearl necklace was absent-mindedly offered the first girl to be presented; the smile that welcomed her curtsy was courteous, nothing more. The other candidates fared no better and no worse. As they filed past, one by one, and the line diminished, a heavy gloom settled over the ministers.

The gifts came to an end just as the last girl stepped forward; there had, no doubt, been some mistake in the count. Unlike the others, this girl looked the Prince full in the face; she held her arms crossed over her bosom and made no attempt to slip down her shawl to reveal her throat. The King, sitting beside his son, saw Siddhartha give a start. She *was* adorable—barely fifteen, and adorable. Suddhodano found himself thinking of Parvati, the radiant daughter of the Himalayas, and of the bride of Siva, and then of a young doe in the mating season, but prudently he kept silent.

"I am Gopa Yasodhara," the girl said simply. And then, smiling, she added, "Is there no gift left for me?"

"There are no more gifts, it is true. But you, whose grace is the pride of our city, shall accept this, instead." As he spoke, the Prince removed the chain of emeralds he wore around his neck and clasped it around the waist of Gopa Yasodhara.

Neither of them spoke, and although their lips were smiling, their eyes were grave. As the seed sprouts from the earth after a long drought, so their former love sprang to life again in an instant. For these two had already been united many times, as man and woman, tiger and tigress, liana and orchid, wind and down, mountain and river. . . . Between them no words were needed: no need for him to recall the deer he had once captured for her in the forest; no need for her to recall the storm that, for thirty-three days, had trapped them, drunk with love, in a cave overhanging the flooded river. So long as the wheel of rebirth turned, so long would that which had been endure within them.

Custom, however, had to be observed, and messengers were solemnly dispatched to Sudrah Dandapani to request the hand of his daughter for the Crown Prince of the Shakyas. And the girl's father submitted in turn to custom. It mattered little, in those days, that the heart spoke, that in a single glance young people pledged themselves to each other for life. By custom, the girl must belong to the most ardent, the most vigorous suitor.

"Neighboring princes have already asked for Gopa Yasodhara's hand—Devadatta, most skillful of archers; Arjuna, the finest of horsemen; Nanda, a master of fencing. And so, O King, if thy son can bend the bow, handle the sword, and tame the wild horse better than they, he will be best in all things and best for us. But will he be able to do this?"

Within the body of the Prince, so harmonious and so disciplined in the games of youth, there dwelled the Bodhisattva who knew everything—even the future. That is to say, Siddhartha knew things, yet did not seem to know them from studying, or by reasoning, or by feeling. Today we would say that intuition governed his actions, words, and thoughts. Therefore, to his father, who was most apprehensive that the heir to the throne might be outclassed by rivals less noble than he, and that he might not be able to welcome Gopa Yasodhara as daughter-in-law into the family of the Shakyas, the young man said cheerfully, "Sudrah Dandapani wishes to give his daughter to a skillful, strong, brave man, and he seems to be afraid that I am only a dreamer who is incapable of defending his people and his rights. But do you—*you*—think that in all Kapilavastu there is a single man who can defeat me? In one week—if it please your lordship—let the most famous among them measure himself against me."

As Gopa Yasodhara sat in the ceremonial chariot prepared for affianced girls—she not yet knowing whose fiancée she would be—she nervously weighed the colossal figure of Nanda, the bulging muscles of Arjuna, the drawn, malevolent face of Devadatta, and the color drained from her cheeks. But then Siddhartha arrived at a gallop on his white horse Kantala. He smiled at her, and leaping to the ground, he cried, "The man who will not today engage all his body and breath is not worthy of this pearl!"

Then the young Prince turned, and he who had seen only Brahmans, courtiers, and palace servants, stared in amazement at the crowd. So *these* were his father's people—differently housed, differently fed than their ruler, yet surely like him in their joys and griefs. The spirit of meditation was about to spread its dark veil over him when the herald summoned him for the archery trial.

Arjuna and Nanda had already pierced both skins of a drum situated about one and a half miles distant. Devadatta had placed his target a hundred yards still farther off and launched an arrow so swift and sure that it seemed impossible to better him. Siddhartha then ordered his drum to be placed a full league away; at that distance, it looked scarcely larger than a sea shell.

Out of courtesy, he asked his cousin to lend him his personal bow, a magnificent weapon fashioned of three sapling trunks lacquered and bound together in a single shaft by the tendons of oxen; it required an uncommon strength even to bend such a weapon. However, with a careless finger, the Prince stretched the silver cord until the tips of the bow touched; with a clap like thunder, the bow snapped in two.

"This is a plaything, it's not for serious use. Is there no more suitable bow for a Shakya nobleman, no weapon worthy of a man?"

Then they brought him the old black bow, encrusted with gold, that, in earlier times, only his ancestor Sinhahanu had been able to bend. For centuries it had been preserved in a temple. The shaft, curved like the horns of the aurochs of the highest plateaus, was as broad as a man's hand. Without apparent effort, without even seeming to take aim, Siddhartha drew back the cord. No one saw the arrow flash forward, but two leagues away old men whose feebleness had kept them at home heard the high-singing vibration of the released cord.

Yasodhara had drawn the end of her sari over her face to hide the fear in her eyes. She could not follow the flight of the arrow, which pierced both skins of the drum and sped onward to double the distance before it buried itself in the ground. A stream of water gushed forth from the spot where it fell and ever since then men have reverenced this natural spring, which they have named the Spring of the Arrow.

With one blow of his saber, Nanda severed a tree trunk six fingers in diameter. Arjuna bettered him by one finger, Devadatta by three. Siddhartha walked over to his father and asked for the loan of the King's dress sword. It was very light, with a slender blade, yet he brandished the weapon with such force that it cut neatly through a double trunk. The two trees remained standing and Nanda was dancing with delight, shouting that the sword had missed the mark; but a puff of wind—assuredly blown by the gods—swept through the foliage and toppled both trees to the ground.

The horse race was uneventful. Kantala ran well ahead of the field and won by several lengths. The disgruntled Nanda went to register a complaint.

"This test proves nothing. Who would not win if he was riding Kantala! Order an unbroken horse fetched and we will see who can make him race once around the track."

It took three grooms, clinging to the halter for dear life, to maneuver the giant stallion to the center of the green meadow. Black as night, with eyes wild and nostrils flaring like crimson pits, he was without saddle or stirrups, for no one had ever risked trying to mount him. Despite his frantic lunging, a groom managed to slip on a bit and two reins. Then the contestants tried their luck.

Nanda kept his seat for five seconds, until the horse bucked a third time, rising straight into the air, with his hoofs tucked under and his back arched. Devadatta clung to the animal's mane when it reared until it was absolutely vertical, but he slipped down its neck and over its head when the stallion lifted its croup high in a mighty kick.

By sawing hard on the bit and lashing the creature's flanks, Arjuna appeared to be subduing it; in a burst of rage and fear, the animal circled the field once, seeming half tamed. But somehow it managed to seize its rider's foot between its teeth, dragged him from its back and shook him furiously. It would have killed him if a groom had not struck it repeatedly and hard on the nose. The apprehensive crowd was shouting, "Do not let Siddhartha have anything to do with this fiend! Its liver roils like a tempest and its blood is like fire!"

But the Prince went up to the horse, gently took hold of its mane, shaded its eyes with his right hand, and talking softly to it, leaped to its back. Its flanks still flecked with foam, the stallion cantered the full length of the track, guided only by the pressure of its rider's knees.

Only Siddhartha presented himself for the tests in reading, reciting, and mathematics, the other contestants having withdrawn. But the examination was canceled, when Vishvamitra hinted to the Brahmans that they risked being made fools of.

Everything was concluded, it seemed, and they were leading over the tall elephant on which the winner was to return in triumph to the palace. But Devadatta, to show his strength, struck it viciously on the trunk and the creature fell.

"You have done a great wrong, cousin."

Siddhartha touched the elephant with his foot; it arose, trumpeted, and then kneeled before him, as if to worship him.

What more could be said after that than what Suddrah Dandapani did say: "Take with thee, O Prince, the treasure thou hast won."

What consent could be more tenderly murmured than Gopa's? Drawing her black veil down over her eyes, she walked gracefully to the victor, and slipping a garland of hibiscus flowers around his neck, leaned her head against his heart.

"Beloved Prince, look upon me, I am thine. Wilt thou accept me as thy wife?"

The language of love is silence, and no one knows what Siddhartha replied.

IV

LONG BEFORE HE HAD SLIPPED HIS EMERALD NECKLACE AROUND Gopa's waist, the Prince had declared to his father: "The girl I marry will be in the springtime of her youth. She will be as beautiful as a flower but not vain. The girl I marry will love all creatures like a sister, like a mother. She will know nothing of bitterness or guile, and she will not be envious. Never, even in her dreams, will she think of any man but her husband. She will never speak haughtily, and she will be as discreet as a slave. The girl I marry will not covet the goods of others, she will not make excessive demands, she will be satisfied with her lot. She will have no taste for strong drink, and she will have no particular relish for fine foods. She will not be a slave to music and she will not use perfume. The girl I marry will be good to her servants; she will be the first to awaken and the last to go to rest. Yes, the girl I marry will be pure in body, in word, and in thought."

King Suddhodano had sighed, reflecting how hard it would be to combine such perfections in a single human being. He had not dared pursue his thought to its conclusion and recommend polygamy. But now he was radiant. For fear that Gopa was actually Maya come back to earth, he could not rest until the marriage should take place, and he asked the astrologers to fix the earliest possible date. Perhaps these two children were a little young. But love, after all, does not wait to count the years.

Never did the rites have to be more strictly observed. The First Minister went to the house of Sudrah Dandapani to state the station and titles of the suitor, to ask in his behalf for the young girl's hand, and when all terms were agreed upon, to seal them with a solemn engagement contract.

History has left no description of the marriage, but it can only have been a ceremony of extraordinary splendor. Led to the royal palace by her attendants, the young bride was symbolically anointed by Siddhartha, who offered her a new robe, the bristle of a porcupine, and a mirror. Bowing low, he then received her from the hand of his father-in-law as a shower of dried barley fell over the young couple. At that point, the Brahmans' role began. They helped Gopa to step up on a stone, to turn seven times about the fire, to make toward each point of the compass the seven steps that irrevocably sealed the union. Before linking the thumbs of bride and groom with a white cotton thread, the Brahmans watched carefully as Siddhartha touched his index finger to the shoulders, the heart, and the navel of the young woman, and then sprinkled sparkling water over her. Lastly, they presided over the giving of lavish presents, for the King had insisted that his gifts be without measure.

Seated side by side on a cushion of gold lamé, with garlands of flowers encircling their heads, the young couple breathed incense-laden air and watched as rice was strewn over the floor. All omens proved propitious: the priests examined the entrails of sacrificial animals; the soothsayers interpreted the flight of birds; the exorcists drove away all evil spirits; the augurs verified an astonishingly favorable conjunction of the stars. Even the two straws set to float on red-tinted milk came together and joined, the evident sign of a love that would last until death.

Seeing how happy the Prince looked, the people were reminded of an old folk expression and said to each other, "There's a boy who doesn't have to hang a pot of boiling water at the foot of his bed and stir it with his toe in order to be loved." And no one took the inevitable crying scene seriously; every young bride owes this to her parents when she leaves them. Was Gopa not like "the liana that embraces the tree"? However, no one remotely guessed that, at that very moment, Yasodhara was remembering a tigress robed in gold and black and a male all bloodied from the battle in which he had endured dreadful blows and clawings in order to keep his jungle companion for himself.

Her husband carried Yasodhara into their apartments, for the foot of a bride dare not touch the threshold of her new home on her wedding day. Siddhartha then took his place opposite her on the hide of a red bull. Each touched the other with the consecrated wafer that they then ate. A tiny male infant, born of a woman who had brought only men children into the world, was placed ceremoniously in Gopa's lap. She then carefully fanned the embers she had brought from her family's house until they burned brightly on her own hearth.

For three successive nights, the couple was obliged to

sleep side by side on the same couch, a boar-spear lying between them. It was the custom for them to unite as man and woman on the fourth day. With a wand, the husband then drove out the demons dwelling in his wife's body, undressed her, and anointed her body, even to fingernails and hair, with scented oils.

In the palace of Vishramvan, which the King had ordered to be built near the capital, Siddhartha came to know pleasure. Sloughing off their indolence for once, masons, tilers, carpenters, and decorators had worked day and night. Within three moons—the exact period of the engagement—everything was finished, the rooms furnished, and the gardens planted. Once again India had brought forth from crude matter one of those miracles of taste and sumptuousness that the passing of time has never completely erased from memory.

It was a palace of far more than a thousand and one enchanted nights, of far more than a thousand and one all too short days. Porticoes of marble, lintels of lazulite, arches of translucent alabaster, doors of wrought cedar opening on shaded apartments, patios with laughing fountains, galleries in which the beauty of the gold leaf rivaled that of the ceramics—all these contributed to its splendor. And how to describe the parks! There was the blue garden, the yellow garden, the rose, and the all-white, each with pools with darting multicolored fish. Over the lawns peacocks unfurled their jeweled tails and young hinds grazed. Fear was banished from these places; the lizard warmed himself in the sun, never scuttling off when a man drew near; squirrels came to eat out of one's hand; green doves, the purple-banded parrots, and the Bengali finches greeted the visitor. It was a miracle of peace; even the monkeys did not bicker with the crows.

And the view! A tumble of blinding white mountain peaks—virgin, infinite, breath-taking—were etched against a blue sky; their lower slopes were covered with green oak and fluted with waterfalls, and at their feet the Rohini flowed across the plain, between willows and aspen, to empty its waters into the holy Ganges. A thousand sounds whispered through the tamarind trees. Siddhartha and his wife loved to single them out: the call of the pheasants, the roar of a marauding panther, the bleating of sheep, the lowing of the work oxen, and now and then the trumpet call of a wild elephant.

What the young Prince did not notice was that, at night, masons and blacksmiths came in furtive haste to construct a triple wall with brass gates. The King was relying on this to isolate his son from any and all temptation. The wall was screened by trees; from the gardens its presence could not be detected, but it was nonetheless there, a solid latch to the gilded cage. The gates were so heavy that it took a hundred men to swing one of them open, and the noise could be heard a mile away. "Let no one pass, not even my son. You shall answer for this with your heads." For that matter, there was no sign that Siddhartha minded being kept in this charming prison, of which love was the jailer and delight the bars; the chains of happiness and pleasure were too short for him to draw near the confines of his domain.

In the heart of the palace was a holy of holies. Here every sound was stilled, every light was softened to leave love and silence undisturbed. It was, indeed, impossible to know whether the light was that of dusk, or of invisible lamps, or of a new dawn; whether the air stirred with the humming of bees or with a muted music. In the bedchamber of the young couple—the most secluded among a hundred other rooms—there flowed perpetually a breeze as fresh as that of a summer night. Light, filtered through panels of mother-of-pearl, cast a suffused iridescence over the silken coverings of the beds. All sound was hushed in furs and rugs of deep-piled wool.

Siddhartha lived in a dream world of pleasure. The moment the Prince awoke, servants came with fans and perfumes to freshen the drowsy cheeks of their young lord. Whatever the hour, they were followed by cupbearers who brought him small cakes and sherbets made of virgin snow from the mountain peaks, and all manner of strength-restoring foods. Dancing girls slipped into his chamber; the tiny bells encircling their wrists and ankles made a strangely stirring, rhythmic accompaniment as the women turned slowly about his couch, their parted robes revealing slender arms and thighs sheathed in gold-flecked voile. They were as light of foot, Siddhartha had been told, as the Apsarases of the gods. The hours slipped by unheeded as he listened to Gopa Yasodhara sing to the murmuring chorus of her ladies' voices. No one noticed if it was day or night as the lutes and the two-stringed violins blended with flute and cithara in impalpable skeins of harmony.

A most astonishing thing in all this was that while the King kept carefully in the background, he was actually directing his son's pleasures. Yet Suddhodano himself was living almost like an ascetic. He forced himself to subdue every impulse of the heart, he denied himself every indulgence, he gave in neither to prodigality nor to avarice. As one tames a wild stallion, so he mastered his senses and lived with the one desire of increasing his knowledge, the better to serve his people. He was never heard to make a cruel—albeit true—comment or to say a kind word that would distort his real opinion.

Devout, disdaining all profane pleasures, Suddhodano seemed to have transferred to the Crown Prince a man's zestful appetite for life. He went even further: by official decree, everything that could evoke age, illness, and death he ordered banished from the palace of Vishramvan. Let a dancer betray a trace of weariness and she was withdrawn; a servant was dismissed if her plaited hair showed a touch of gray. A faded flower or a dead leaf was taboo. No lamp could flicker low for lack of oil.

The ruler of the Shakyas had not forgotten his son's stunned dismay when the young man discovered how the laughing spectacle of nature hides violent death, destruction, and pain. Also, he remembered the prophecy of the Brahmans: "If he does not agree to reign, your son will rend your very entrails." Hopefully he kept thinking, if his youth is spent far from the things that stir up thought and hatch the sterile eggs of reflection, maybe the shadow of a destiny too vast for any human will fade away. . . . However, a contrary dream often wrenched the sovereign awake in a sweat of anguish.

His anxiety was lightened the day he overheard the servants indiscreetly gossiping that, perhaps, a happy event . . . To this child, scarcely yet a promise—and a boy, beyond any question—he said to himself he would give the lilting name of Rahula. Beyond any question, also, Siddhartha would now reign in order to pass down the throne to his own son, as all kings do. A happy man does not abandon an adored wife, a child, and a dynastic succession just to go running after adventure.

Destiny, however, was there. And four times it was to knock on the brass gates of Vishramvan.

Book Three

I

ONE EVENING—AN EVENING LIKE ALL OTHER EVENINGS IN THAT
marvelous palace where sensual delights were so palpable that
one longed to caress them like warm turtledoves—one evening, then, Gopa danced for her husband. The music was a
melodious whispering that one listened to dreamily, noticing neither tune nor rhythm. A gourd hung in a doorway,
suspended from silver cords, and it sighed as the fitful wind
played on it. Conches, vinas, flat drums, kettledrums, flutes,
and cymbals—and even the brass drum, that usually bellows
so, and the squirmingly shrill hautboy—merged into a sinuous harmony in which one could identify no single voice.

Gopa was happy. Happy because she had learned from a

young but experienced matron that a new life was forming within her. Happy because that night she was wearing the white gown, embroidered with precious stones, and the necklace of red coral presented to her by the King. Happier still, perhaps, because of her father-in-law's retort to certain straitlaced critics who had censured her going out with her face unveiled: "My son and my daughter are pure. Their union is like the blending of cream and milk."

On a divan draped with cloth soft and silky as the nose of a she-ass, Siddhartha sat in smiling absorption. He did not smile, however, because he was watching Gopa as she danced for his delight; he was listening to voices that, although inaudible to the others, resounded in his head like the humming sea-sounds of a shell pressed to the ear:

> "Deliver all creatures from their suffering,
> "Show patience with respect to the hundred
>   worlds;
> "Lord of those who go on two feet, depart
>   and accomplish thy mission. Release the
>   rains of deliverance."

His eyes had closed, but not in sleep. They were turned inward on curious visions: a prince who had been martyred by a reigning rival of his father's was watching a trickle of milk flow from his severed ankles; the king of the antelopes was bounding before a hunter in order to guide the man to a ford; a she-bear was giving suck to a peasant trapped in a cave by the heavy snows; a wild elephant was helping a man who had tried to capture it, to free himself from some sharp brambles. Siddhartha did not doubt that it was he himself—he the martyred prince, the antelope, she-bear, elephant—who had lived these experiences. In the same way, he felt that his own body was only an envelope offered to some Other Being who dwelled in it and thought and acted under the name of Siddhartha. But this Other Being had not yet made itself openly known to him.

What suffering, what creatures had those voices been speaking of? Knowing nothing of pain, of age, of grief, or of death, the Prince struggled to find some meaning in the summons. His nights were turbulent and when he awoke, he felt as if he were returning exhausted from a dark voyage. Sometimes, with his eyes still closed and his face haggard, he would start up in his bed, crying "O my world, my world! I am coming!," and only the lips of Gopa could calm him.

Presently he was tormented by a driving desire to see these creatures at first hand. He sensed that the world held more than the cloud of gracious young women surrounding him, who could sometimes be so intolerably attentive, and the noble, bearded courtiers who were so proud of the saber symbolizing their caste, or the slaves whom he knew only by sight of their knobby spines. (One day, when his father was giving an audience to an envoy from the kingdom of Magadha, he had overheard the two men speak of fields ravaged by drought, of famine, and children dying of starvation.) And so he decided to go out into the world beyond the palace. After all, had this ever been forbidden him?

A driver came to warn Suddhodano that the Prince had ordered him to harness his bullocks. "Good!" the King said, approvingly. "Better to clip the falcon's wings now."

Since the Prince and his retinue had to cross the city, the King ordered heralds to ring bells and beat drums so that by evening the streets should be cleared of every upsetting sight. No heaps of filth were to be visible, no beggars or cripples, no butcher's blocks where the meat disappeared under a cloud of flies, no chained slave gangs digging ditches, no scavengers bent under their heavy slop barrels, no funeral processions.

The orders were promptly obeyed, and, at the same time, with a speed rare in a country disposed to be leisurely, banners and oriflammes and parasols were unfurled, grassy banks were embellished with flowers, silken draperies were hung from house walls, bouquets of flowers brightened window sills, streets were sprayed with delicate perfumes, and homeowners dusted red sand before the doorways of their dwellings. Only then, as the metallic groan of the hinges mingled with the panting of a hundred slaves straining against the heavy doors, was the great eastern gate opened wide.

When the Prince arrived, at a trot, in his chariot drawn by two white bullocks, the capital wore a holiday air. Pots of smoldering basil leaves poured forth a light, fragrant cloud that blurred all details. It was a vision, a dream! And a scene of unmarred happiness, too. Massed against the walls of the houses, the people showed only laughing faces as they shouted themselves hoarse—their cheers were heartfelt, for that matter, for they had a spontaneous love for the Prince, if only because of his radiant youth. The avenues lay broad and straight before his chariot, and had been reserved for his passage alone. The principal artery of Kapilavastu was, accordingly, entirely empty except . . .

except for an old man who suddenly came out of a doorway that as suddenly disappeared. We, who now know so many secrets, can surmise that that door appeared there briefly by will of the Bodhisattva. Perhaps the old man was the Archangel himself. Everyone knows that a god can double, can triple himself, as he likes; he can be several people at the same time and in the same place or in different places.

If, indeed, this figure was Avalokiteshvara, he had assumed the repulsive form of a man in the last stages of physical decay. To further the ends of destiny, he had made himself feeble and completely bald; his muscles were stringy and lined with bulging, pulpy veins through which the nearly dried blood flowed sluggishly. Saliva dribbled down his chin, and when he opened his mouth and spat, his few remaining teeth waggled; from time to time he uttered hoarse, guttural grunts. The skin across his belly was so finely wrinkled that it could be mistaken for crepe. He supported his tottering carcass on a cane, and he was mumbling, "Alms, good people, alms, or I will be dead tomorrow."

"*What* is that?" the Prince asked, with horror, before the guards could hustle this human offal out of sight.

"Just a man beset by old age, my lord," his driver Chana turned around to answer. "Very likely he was once handsome, strong, and loved. And, what's more, probably very rich. But now that he is more than eighty years old, his relatives despise him because he can no longer guide the family fortunes, and the young women of the household are revolted by him. But his grandchildren will soon lead him into the forest and abandon him there, with a beggar's wallet filled with food. Because he is an offense, an offense to the eye and to the mind."

"Aaah? . . . Is that the law in his family or for everyone?"

"Your Highness is pleased to joke! . . . The King your father, your aunt the Lady Maha Prajapati, your wife, who is said to be so beautiful—you yourself, my lord, will grow old like that. And I can't pass over myself, if the gods grant me long life."

But, like smoke dispersed by the winds, the old man had disappeared.

It was a thoughtful and disturbed Siddhartha who again slipped out of the palace, this time by the southern gate. He had put on a merchant's garb, while his driver Chana was disguised as a water carrier. In the course of the distressed night the Prince had spent after returning from his first sortie, he had come to understand that the world is not full only of holiday clothes and agreeable faces. This time, he had decided to forego his chariot and to travel on foot.

He had never dreamed of such a sight as now spread before his eyes! Merchants were standing among heaps of grain and spices, money-changers were wrangling, broad-necked street porters stumbled under their loads, and bearers balancing great palanquins chanted to keep in step. Inside the houses the weavers' shuttles clattered; cows grazed shamelessly among the fruits on the open stalls; the sweetshop was abuzz with flies; the dyers spread their scarves, dripping trickles of colored water, out to dry. And the crowds! All those chattering women and men intent on their work; and the asses and horses and carts. How many children, too! Some were attending an open-air school led by a Brahman; some, open-mouthed and deliciously terrified, were watching the head of a cobra sway as it listened, charmed, to a double flute. And the strange odors! Pungent smells from open-air kitchens—whiffs of tumeric and of fish rotting in the sun, of charred wood and savory herbs—mingled with smoke that made the eyes smart, and with the fumes of dung and incense in the temple, and the stench of human sweat. And the noise! The air rang with a medley of cries, shouts, and songs that still could not drown out the measured hammering of iron hot on the anvil or the whole scale of sounds produced by mallets as they tapped, tapped, tapped on brass and wood and leather and stone.

Siddhartha did not hide his amusement—or the slight nagging uneasiness he felt. So these were the busy people whose destinies his father guided, these were the men and women he himself would someday have to lead? At one point, he decided that he could never dream of ascending the throne before learning how to work in metal and in wood, how to bear heavy burdens, how to spend days on end in a shop, crouched like a spider in its web, awaiting the entrance of a customer. Could a man imagine managing the affairs of people he did not know?

He had reached this point in his reflections when, in the center of a circle of loiterers who kept themselves prudently at a distance, he saw a man lying on the ground. He had apparently fallen there and no longer had the strength to get up or even to push away his own excrement that befouled the litter he lay on. A man in the prime of life, clearly, but as clearly sick and emaciated, whose face was convulsed by the onslaughts of pain. He was breathing with difficulty, and his hand moved ceaselessly to finger the huge bubo that swelled his groin; even before touching the infected place, he could not keep from groaning.

"That man, my lord, is begging death to deliver him, but actually he suffers more from fear of death, which is near, than he does from his sickness."

Siddhartha had kneeled, and resting the unhappy man's head against his thigh, he had loosened his own scarf and was gently wiping away the sweat that poured down the man's face.

"Oh, master," the driver moaned, "it's bad, bad to hold him like that. You can catch his sickness! Look how those people shy away from him. People are so afraid that he has the plague and will pass it on to them that he has no more friends, no place to go, not even a physician. . . . People don't care much for people who are dangerously sick, you know!"

"Oh, Chana, Chana, are there many like this? Could it happen to me? Could I suddenly be struck down by the same sickness? . . . Suddenly, or little by little?"

But before the driver had time to explain that illness does not distinguish rich man from poor and that it knocks at every door, the plague-ridden man had disappeared and an open parasol sparkled gaily in the sunlight, sheltering a flower girl from the temple of Indra.

The distraught, tormented Prince knew no peace until the northern gate had opened before his chariot. Once again, all was gaiety in the city, and the excursion was nearly ended, having greatly eased Siddhartha's heart, when the bullocks flinched.

A funeral procession was crossing the street. A litter of matted boughs supported a body tightly wrapped in a shroud. Weeping relatives followed on foot, the women moaning, with their disheveled hair streaming down their shoulders; the men gathered up fistfuls of dust, which they flung over their heads.

"Ah, now that man, my lord, has nothing left—neither relatives nor children nor friends nor home. Soon the flames of the pyre will consume him and he will no longer have even a body. And in four generations not one of his descendants will remember that he ever existed."

Siddhartha stepped down from his chariot and followed the procession on foot. It was as if he were magnetized; he could not turn his eyes from the pyre, encircled by leaping tongues of fire, or from the body, which sat up, suddenly, in the midst of the flames and then fell back in an explosion of sparks. The aroma of spices and sandalwood was soon overpowered by the smell of burning flesh, and the Prince was assailed by nausea. Yet he waited until the greasy smoke had floated away and until the ashes had cooled so that, joining with the other watchers, he could pluck from the residue a few crumbling bones that were then pulverized between stones.

"Tell me, Chana, is this how all living things end?"

The driver shrugged. "The body must be destroyed, so it's as well for it to be burned as to be given over to filthy worms. The moment the light is spent . . ."

"Back to the palace, driver, quickly! . . . Oh, woe to youth that surrenders to age, woe to health that is struck down by disease! Woe, woe, woe to the path along which the wise man can do no more than pass!"

Morose, silent, and wan, the Prince cast a pall over the Vishramvan palace for more than a month. The dancing girls went spiritlessly through the motions of their dances, the musicians were distracted, the pastry cooks lost their touch. Even the waxen torches cast a funereal light. Siddhartha both wanted and did not want to go out. No sooner were the white bullocks with their gilded horns yoked to his chariot than he gave orders for them to be unharnessed, and he fled to shut himself up far away from everyone. Far away even from Gopa, who wept in her apartments not so much from grief as because she could not understand what she was guilty of that her husband should neglect her so.

Finally, Siddhartha could hold out no longer. Ordering the western gate to be opened, he seized the reins himself and drove the chariot toward the setting sun. Very soon the bullocks stopped, of their own volition, tossing their heads with obvious joy. A young monk, calm and serene, was holding out his begging bowl in a gesture of simple dignity.

"Who is that man? He seems so deeply happy."

"A bhikshu, my lord. A wandering monk."

"Ah! Now there is a man who could grow old, fall sick and die, yet he makes you feel that nothing could ever destroy his peace of heart. What do you think, driver? To be a monk —is that the way to find help?"

Without parting his firmly closed lips or even moving

them, the Bodhisattva—for it was he in the guise of a yellow-clad monk—spoke in a penetrating voice: "Man finds ultimate help for himself by helping others."

Chana was living in a state of torment. The Prince had violated the code of his Kshatriya caste; he had defiled himself by touching a sick man, mingling with mourners, handling burnt bones; in short, he had behaved like any vile outcast. And so, although he feared he might lose his head, the driver went to inform the King of his son's recent doings; he passed over the defilements, however, in silence. When Suddhodano pressed him to learn more, he became evasive.

"Maybe I was dreaming, Sire. Maybe we didn't meet anyone, maybe my young master didn't ask . . . Oh, surely that must be the way it was. The guards Your Majesty has stationed along all the streets would have seen something, too, wouldn't they? . . . But it is strange how my lord keeps talking about the peace of being a monk. And about helping all living creatures . . ."

Suddhodano was a man of decision. That very evening, the walls of the palace compound were reinforced by a thick spiny hedge; a patrol route was established, along which elephants and chariots moved steadily. While on duty, guards wore armor and carried pikes. In a word, the palace geared itself for war against an enemy the King himself could not have identified.

Simultaneously, orders were issued that, at all costs, joy must reign in the palace; indeed, the King came in person to impress his instructions upon the women. "You will not interrupt your games and your singing for an instant. Offer him every pleasure you know. Intoxicate my son, charm him with every voluptuous delight until he loses this notion of becoming a religious."

Despite these energetic orders, gloom fell like ashes over

Vishramvan. Geese, swans, peacocks, jays, parakeets drooped and turned silent. The lotus in the pools did not flower, branches about to burst into blossom withered. The strings of the viols snapped when struck by the bow, and the skins of the drums sagged at the touch of a finger.

One morning, as dawn was brightening the milky translucence of the alabaster windows, a distraught Gopa burst into the bedchamber where Siddhartha had decided, a month earlier, to sleep alone. She was a charming and desirable young woman, in her long tunic of crimson voile; her hair, as sootily dark as the black bee, fell in heavy curls over her shoulders.

"My sweet lord, I am angry with myself for coming to disturb your rest. And I would not have broken in on your solitude, if my own unhappiness had not driven me to confide in you. . . . I have just had a dream. The earth was trembling, and the sun, the moon, and the stars were falling over the tops of the mountains. I was naked, and I saw that my body had lost every sign of being female. My hair was all tangled, and my crown had fallen to the stone floor. You were there, and so was your father, and all our rich robes were flying through the air in tatters. The royal umbrella snapped cleanly halfway down the handle. Presently, flames shot up from the city, an immense sheet of water rolled over the plain and, as I watched, Mount Meru began to sway. . . . Then everything changed. I was all alone, dressed in a white robe, and the Nagas and Rakshasas were bowing down before me. . . . Explain all this to me, my heart's master, and drive my fears away. I feel there is some terrible mystery in this dream."

For the first time in weeks, Siddhartha smiled. His eyes shone like polished onyx in the shadows of his bedchamber. He stroked Gopa's long curling hair, and speaking slowly and carefully, he said, "Don't let these visions upset you. The broken royal umbrella—well, I myself dreamed that I was an umbrella, an umbrella that sheltered the whole world. The fire of your dream was consuming the corruption of cities, the ocean was drowning error. But I needn't belabor the dream's message. . . . And it doesn't matter that our princely robes were ripped, because the day will come when we will have only our virtues to clothe us. Ah! Actually, the omens in your dream are favorable!"

She was laughing now, happy to have found her husband again. She asked archly, "Yet in the beginning I was quite naked. And with nothing of a woman—"

"Of course, Gopa, of course. It means that one day you will have nothing more to do with a woman's body."

For the moment, in any case, her garment was still intact, and its filmy texture revealed forms entirely feminine. And since, before adopting a monk's estate, Siddhartha would have to ask permission of his father and king, and since both were young and united as are milk and cream, the Prince finished by falling asleep on the shoulder of Gopa Yasodhara whose tender fingers lightly fanned his closed eyes.

Moon followed upon moon. The Prince gave no further sign of intending to leave the palace, and the guard was roundly bored because there was no enemy to fight. "*Mudra?*" the sentry cried, without conviction. "*Angana,*" came the listless reply. Drums beat out the changes of the guard and were promptly reconverted to dice tables.

One night, unable to sleep, Siddhartha got up and strolled slowly through the gardens, circling the pools that the moon had washed with silver. He was mulling over the dreams that his father, Gopa Yasodhara, and one of the young court ladies had confided to him, and the dreams that he himself had salvaged from sleep because of their intensity—indeed, there had been a vast amount of dreaming in the palace during the last few months. He could, of course, interpret all of them, not only the galloping of a marvelous horse that had borne his wife off toward that land of the pale-skinned men where the sun vanished below the horizon of a boundless sea, but also the seven visions of the King, in which Indra's flag with its golden sun floated, in tatters, above ten elephants, while a tower rose to the heavens, a mighty drum resounded, and a glittering wheel revolved, with a flashing of jewels, around six men who sat plunged in despair.

Were these not eloquent dreams that were deliberately sent so that they might be repeated to the Prince? Beyond the interpretations that his heart divined rather than his mind analyzed, were the dreams not also warning Siddhartha that the moment had come for him to leave the flowery path leading inexorably to illness, old age, and death, and to follow the uneven path of Wisdom?

His restless steps had brought the Prince to the royal palace. The brightness that accompanied him was so intense that it shone through the closed eyelids of the sleeping Suddhodano. The King blinked, dazzled by the light that glinted from the bare walls of the cell where he was sleeping.

"Ho there, eunuch! Is the sun already up?"

"No, no, Master, no. If this were the dawn's light, Your Majesty would also feel the heat."

But Siddhartha was already standing before his father, radiating the assurance of unshakable joy. The Holy Writings have handed down to us a splendid speech, at once respectful and firm, logically persuasive, abloom with metaphors, bedecked with more poetic images than there were finches in the royal aviary. It was, all the same, a trifle long, and we can safely confine ourselves to his closing words: "Therefore, O King, O my father, grant—and with you, all your family and all your people—grant that I may go my way."

Suddhodano had clearly heard such words as "deliverance . . . sufferings of others . . . frightful cycle of exist-

ences . . . supreme royalty . . ." but could not make any
sense out of them. He shook his head as if to chase away flies.

"Is there something you want? Royalty, you say? This
palace, the servants, the kingdom—take them all. But stay
among us!"

For a long while Siddhartha stood plunged in a silent
reverie.

"Indeed, my lord, perhaps I could remain here always,
with a smile on my lips and joy in my heart. So, grant me not
all this wealth but four things, four simple things: that old
age never take possession of me; that the flush of youth live
always on my cheeks; that illness never ravage my body; that
my life continue without declining for all time. . . . When I
say *I, my* cheeks, *my* body, *my* life, I also mean you and Gopa
and all those who live in the palace and beyond it. . . .
Otherwise, I must leave before the full moon."

Far from giving up, Suddhodano felt the fighting spirit
of a true Kshatriya boil in his veins. At each of the four brass
gates of Vishramvan, he stationed five hundred young nobles
commanding chariots supported by foot soldiers. We will not
enumerate all the troops reported by history, for they would
exceed the number of men then available throughout all the
kingdoms of India. Every corner, every square, every main
street was guarded by brothers and cousins of the King. All
wandering monks were ordered to the frontiers of the kingdom. There were four critical days before the moon would
be full.

For her part, Maha Prajapati Gautami called the women
and slaves together.

"Rekindle all the fires. No light is to be allowed to go
out, day or night. Music will be played constantly to keep
awake anyone who is overcome by sleep. You can sleep next
week. . . . You will not let your Prince out of your sight for

an instant. Use every woman's charm you know, captivate him until body and soul are enchanted and he forgets about wanting to go away to become a bhikshu."

Siddhartha could not take a step without running into dancing girls. Wide-eyed with admiration, they would surround him and, cupping their hands like the calyx of the anemone, they would murmur in seemingly astonished confusion, "But here is the god of love, here is Kama in person." Even Uyadin, a boyhood companion of the Prince's, was ordered by the King to intervene in the weaving of this silken net. He instructed various young women of the court in special arts to ensnare Siddhartha. But most of them relied on the instinct of their sex and preferred to trust their own imaginations. Some seemed to have accidentally sipped a drop too many of palm wine; others contrived to brush by thickets so that the thorns rent the filmy silks that veiled their young bodies; still others swung languidly on the lianas or sang songs that whispered of the secret desires of springtime.

And, to excuse a gesture or word that ordinarily would have flouted Brahmanic decorum, each young woman kept repeating to herself the royal command: "Watch over the Prince as if he were a butterfly poised for flight."

The five Jinas, guardians of the cardinal points, had, quite naturally, not turned away from their eternal meditations, but their spiritual reflections had brightened and were in communication. Although not directly consulted, the thirty-three gods had, from their paradise, made known their opinion also. In order to snatch Siddhartha from the King's surveillance, they proposed dispatching the five hundred fearsome yakshas to annihilate Suddhodano's troops. Indra even offered the support of his irresistible ten arms for the enterprise. The two wives of Vishnu suggested honoring the fugitive by strewing flowers along the roads, unfurling banners and parasols in the luminous night, and spraying the air with perfumes. Brahma spoke up for a seven-tiered chariot studded with precious stones; the king of the Nagas favored a palace thirty-two leagues in girth, to be put up in a few hours. . . . All of these offers, obviously, came from powerful persons accustomed to using force and to living in luxury.

Time, the master of the gods, shrugged. "It will be no harder to remove Siddhartha, were he as heavy as Mount Meru or imprisoned three leagues below the earth, than it is for the wax bill to snap up a grain of rice. He will leave on his own. . . . I will take care of strengthening his will by showing him how time ravages the most beautiful and most precious things. As for the rest of you, see to it that everything that breathes falls asleep and that every sound is muffled."

In Vishramvan, the lamps flickered and died as if they had been blown out; voices were abruptly stilled; the tambourins and flutes subsided into silence. The sudden quiet and the darkness aroused the Prince. Leaving his couch, he studied the forms of women lying on rugs on the great paving stones and lighted only by a moonbeam slanting through the windows.

"Am I in a charnel house!"

They were a fearful sight. These bodies that had been so charming in their youthfulness the evening before were now stricken with the stigmas of the last stages of physical decay. Their rich robes were in rags, their once flashing jewels had grown dull, their bodies looked flaccid or shriveled, their proud bosoms sagged limply, their lips were drawn back to disclose gaping holes between their broken teeth, their silky, carefully groomed hair had thinned and turned coarse and gray and matted. What had become of the lovely bronze skin, petal-soft to the touch, the nimble hands with hennaed palms, the elegant throats modeled to wear precious necklaces, all the delicate treasures that woman pretends to hide the better to sharpen a man's desire to discover them?

Siddhartha stepped over these ravaged figures with distaste and strode quickly toward Gopa's bedroom. Lifting the blue silk curtain that screened the carved sandalwood doorway, he paused, hesitating to climb the three marble steps: What new horror would he find?

His bare feet sank into carpets like beds of flowers as he advanced cautiously. He had no eyes for the walls of lapis lazuli encrusted with pearls, for the coffered ceiling from which the red bowls of the oil lamps hung, casting a warm glow over the jasper tiles of the floor; he did not notice the fusion of spices, musk, and flowers that enfolded him in waves of perpetually shifting scent. He had eyes only for the couch where Gopa lay, her breathing, in sleep, like a soft purr.

She was as beautiful now as in the first, wonderful days of their marriage. Her shawl had slipped to her waist, revealing her amber body. Her unbound hair lay curled, like a black serpent, between her breasts. One hand was holding a rose; the other hung lightly over the side of the bed, and the moon fastened a bracelet of light around the emeralds at her wrist. Siddhartha leaned over the lovely face; with his finger he traced the line of her eyebrow, smiled at the pearls her parted lips disclosed. He straightened up swiftly when he heard his sleeping wife murmur, "Is it you, my life?"

Now, sitting on the cool tiles, with eyes closed, he was following the thoughts and the dreams of Gopa Yasodhara: she was watching a bull ram a barrier and shoulder past some guards; the flag of Indra, floating over a fortress, was rent and gave way to a silver-threaded banner that fluttered gently in the early morning breeze. Then the young woman was

looking sadly at an empty pillow and a tunic that lay on her
bed; her couch turned over, her belt of pearls slipped off and
turned into a serpent that kept biting her; her bracelets fell
in pieces, and her jasmine crown was pulverized to dust.
"The time has come," she sighed.

An extraordinary light, almost a phosphorescence, bathed
the face of Siddhartha. He was himself and his young wife,
simultaneously, and he no longer distinguished his own body
from hers. He could not help smiling at a tremor that stirred
her . . . his . . . womb, and he arose. "Yes, the time has
come. But will I be able to go? Will I be able to leave you
and our child? . . . If not now, then surely never."

For a long time he stood by the bed. The moon climbed
high into the sky until its almost vertical rays scarcely penetrated the room. Wordlessly, by thought alone, the Prince
was conveying to his wife that he must wrest from heaven—
or from hell—the secret of man's deliverance. His heart beat
in unison with all those hearts that were suffering in the world
outside, and he felt within him the strength, which only a man
at the peak of happiness can possess, to undertake a task from
which even the gods had turned away, knowing that they
were impotent to save anyone from affliction.

The moonlight had vanished entirely from the room.
Siddhartha looked tenderly at his wife's sleeping face and saw
that a tiny tear was drying on her cheek. He kneeled, touched
his forehead to her feet, and walked three times around her
bed, his hands joined, exactly as a Brahman moves around an
altar. Then, drawing his scarf over his head, he went quickly
from the room, his step one of irrevocable decision.

Outside, the errant wind caressed the fluttering fringe of
his robe, the stars twinkled, and the flowers unfolded to welcome him with their perfume. The earth, stirred by hope,

trembled, and the air was filled with music; four rosy dawns glowed at the four cardinal points, paling the moon that now rode at its zenith. High in the arching heavens, Pushya, the Prince's lucky star, sparkled like a fiery jewel.

At the sound of his master's light step, the equerry Sankala—who never slept really soundly—leaped to his feet.

"Saddle Kantala, take a horse for yourself, and come back here."

"Is my lord thinking of riding at night in the gardens?"

"Hush! Be quiet and be quick. The time has come for me to leave this bediamonded cage and seek the Truth. For the sake of man's well-being I must find it."

The equerry was so stunned that, in a total lapse of etiquette, he squatted down on his heels.

"It's true, then! That chatterbox of a driver has been telling the truth? You do want to take the begging bowl of a monk and wander through the world with all its dangers? Oh, my lord, think of the King's affliction, the grief of Madame Gopa, the sorrow of us all. How can you talk about helping people and, in the same breath, desert them? . . . No, master, enjoy the pleasures of life a while longer. Learn to know the child who will soon be born, carry him to the temple, present him to the gods, give him brothers. . . . Later, when your beard has grown gray, when your arms are less strong but your mind is strengthened by experience, then place your eldest son on the throne and go to meditate in the forest. You can find the way to save us all from suffering then."

Even as he was speaking Sankala heard a reply not through his ears but inside his head.

"Desires are neither constant nor lasting. Like the void that misleads the blind man, they are without substance. Like the bowl of unbaked clay, they break when one offers or grasps them. Like salt water, they make one thirst to drink more. . . . It is a false love that attaches us to a loved one in the hope of winning joy."

Clasping his head, Sankala wept.

"Where will you go, O Prince among men?" The simple groom spoke with a sincerity and fervor that made his words sing. "You of the sweeping brows and eyes beautiful as the petals of the lotus, you are like the full autumn moon, like the white lotus rejoicing in the moon's mild light. Your face is like the flower caressed into bloom by the dawn. You shine like pure gold, sparkle like the diamond, flash like the lightning. You move with the sure step of the elephant, the virile bearing of the bull. You who are as proud as a lion, as elegant as a swan—where, where will you go, master?"

When the equerry finally understood that a deluge of pikes, axes, arrows, and flaming iron could fall like the monsoon, that the mountains could catch fire and the seas flood the fields but that the Prince's will would not waver, he ran, groaning, toward the stables.

Kantala always liked to be harnessed; he knew that the silver bit, the reins, and a snugly adjusted saddle meant a grand gallop between his master's knees. He whinnied now with pleasure as the equerry lengthened the gold stirrups and threw a silk caparison over his back. He whinnied more loudly still, his scarlet nostrils flaring, when Siddhartha firmly bestrode him and grasped the reins in his hands. Everyone would have jumped, had the palace not been sunk in sleep.

"Quiet, my white Kantala, quiet. And now take me on my way, on the longest journey that ever rider undertook."

The two horses did not clatter over the paving stones because the gods slipped little cushions of down under their iron shoes. The three elephants did not have to push open the bronze doors with their foreheads; the doors opened by themselves, making no more noise than a swarm of hornets. Neither the guards nor their officers stirred, plunged as they all were in a sleep as profound as the torpor induced by the poppy seeds of Malwa.

Siddhartha had ridden only a short distance when he reined Kantala in. Stroking the horse's neck, he turned in his saddle to look down at the capital, which lay in the valley, its roofs glinting under the rays of the setting moon.

"Not before I have won an end to birth and to death will I enter this city again. Nor before I have achieved the supreme state that is exempt from old age and death, nor before I have acquired Pure Wisdom. When I return, Kapilavastu will stand erect; it will not be bowed down in sleep."

The gods had gathered at the cardinal points. In the east, the Ghandarvas were playing the vina and the harp; the Nagas exhaled perfumed vapors in the west. To the north, vases breathed a smoking incense while, to the south, the yakshas held flaming torches aloft. Music had struck up that no human ear could hear; from the sky flowers were cascading that no young girl would ever gather up to entwine in her hair; fragrances that no human nose could detect scented the air. All earthbound life seemed suspended.

Only the sleeping birds plumped their feathers, thinking drowsily that in an hour they would be singing to greet the return of the sun.

The morning star had risen above the horizon to the height of half a lance and a light breeze was beginning to flow over the land as the two riders reached the steep bank of the river Anoma, which swept along the frontier of the kingdom. Siddhartha leaned forward over the neck of his horse, kissed him between the ears, and jumped down.

He spread his purple mantle on the ground, and upon it he placed his five-stranded collar of pearls, the smallest of which was larger than a hazelnut; the three heavy bracelets of gold, which encircled his forearm; the enameled girdle on which the figures of the gods had been worked; his sword, and his dagger. He took off, also, his earrings, each fashioned of a cabochon ruby trembling at the end of a gold chain, and his medallion. Lastly, he unwound his turban of princely egret feathers and laid beside it the three combs of blond tortoise shell that secured his plaited hair.

"You take my horse back," he said simply. "Take good care of him; he's brought me where I had to come to begin my mission."

Then, stripped of his splendor, he picked up his sword, drew it from its scabbard and carefully cut off the braid he had unwound from about his head. Sankala's mouth twisted with chagrin as the blade cut through the hair, but it gaped in amazement as the beribboned tresses, thrown negligently aside, did not fall to the ground but seemed to be caught up by invisible hands; they rose toward the sky in a halo of light until they disappeared in a gold casket Indra was holding open to receive them. So true is this story that, in later days, the faithful built a stupa on the site of the miracle.

A shadow of discontent clouded Siddhartha's face. He considered his clothing with vexation; it was still far too rich to suit a vagabond who would have to get his food from charity. Yet he hesitated to denude himself entirely, like a yogi. At that moment, a hunter emerged from the thicket. We today who know all about the miraculous story can say definitely that, once again, the Bodhisattva Avalokiteshvara had favored the plans of his earthly incarnation by creating this timely but ephemeral personage.

An exchange of clothing was proposed and—naturally —immediately accepted. The man's clothing was green and rust, the colors of the leaves of the forest; it was a little torn by thorns, a little faded by the rains, perfectly adequate yet sufficiently poor for its wearer to travel the highways and beg for food without attracting attention. In the twinkling of an eye, the hunter, now handsomely clad, disappeared into the brake, while the Prince slipped into his breeches and tunic.

One last time the Prince caressed Kantala, who lowered his head to lick his master's bare feet. Then, without turning back, Siddhartha walked alone into the pathless forest.

Thus transpired the historic event, which, later, came to be called the Great Departure. He who had been the hope of the Shakya clan was now no more than simple Gautama—Gautama the beggar in search of the Truth.

Book Four

I

WITH A SERENE HEART, GAUTAMA PLUNGED INTO FORESTS, crossed plains, skirted the irrigation canals that squared into checkerboard pattern the inundated fields of rice. He was wholly unconcerned whether his path lay in shade or was devoured by the sun. He was full only of the future; he had closed the door of memory behind him and banished everything from his mind except his vision of the suffering the simple fact of existence inflicted upon mankind. He did not even envisage the dismay that must be reigning in Kapilavastu.

The heavens knew, however, what turmoil rocked the palace of Vishramvan when the Prince's disappearance was discovered. Consternation swept over the women, and, as one historian has put it, the women's quarters resembled "a cackling barnyard whose cock has flown." "My brother!" "My lord!" "My friend!" "My master!" they cried, in anguish. And some, blushing, whispered softly, "My beloved!" Women wandered through the gardens, languishing like gazelles pierced by poisoned arrows and seeking only a place where they might die. Others tore their hair, scratched their cheeks, threw themselves headlong on the ground—yet not too violently, for "He" might, after all, return. By evening, his departure seemed a fact. Exhaustion followed on their frenzy; bewitching ladies in waiting and charming slaves sank down wearily by the borders of the pools, like fish fainting from lack of water. Maha Prajapati wept unconsolably— for the King, for the kingdom, for herself. Above all, for Siddhartha, whom she had raised. She stared through her tears at his jewels, which Sankala had brought back to her until, rising abruptly, she ran into the gardens and threw them in a pool.

As for Gopa Yasodhara, she still thought only of Rahula, the son whom Siddhartha would not be able to present at the temple; her fierce grief over losing her husband would come later.

By steady stages, Gautama was nearing the city of Vaisali. He was going there with a very specific purpose, for he had heard tell of Arada Kayala, the most learned Brahman of the kingdom, and wished to become his pupil. Far from receiving the young pilgrim condescendingly, the holy man not only accepted him as disciple among the hundred or so pupils of the Samkhya sect who thronged his ashrama but he offered the young man hospitality without limit. And that same day Gautama attended the lesson.

Intently—and with some surprise—he listened for the first time as a Brahman revealed the speculative ideas developed by his caste. It was a subtle and mysterious philosophy, which Gautama's father, like a good Kshatriya, rather disdained. In the words of the venerable Arada, the Atman, the life principle, the eleventh of the vital breaths to enter the human body, assumes its true aspect as the spiritual essence of all beings and all things; the Atman is unity, is not to be associated with the purely human, and lies behind a diversity and duality that are only apparent.

"When the drum is beaten, who can seize its sound? But if one seizes the drum or the man who plays it, then its sound has been seized."

What the holy man had to say of Brahman as Supreme Being or Ultimate Reality astonished his new disciple no less. He spoke of the connection between the universe and the essential substance of an individual as if he himself had had first-hand experience of it. Without hesitation, he nimbly enumerated the fifteen ways whereby man can communicate with all created beings. He explained that the purpose of sacrifice is purely to escape from this world and to achieve contact with the Universal Force.

Gautama was too impatient to listen any longer. He understood, of course, that everything in the structure of Indian society could be traced back to vegetable life, to the rhythms of nature, the changing of the seasons, the unfolding of time. He accepted, albeit with reservations, the view that during his earthly stay man existed primarily as a member of the collectivity and must submit to its exigencies. But when Arada spoke of the gods, he could not contain himself, and he spoke up.

There was general stupefaction. What was this? A mere youth of twenty-nine was daring to discuss what a venerable white-haired man had spent many years striving to understand, so that he might explain it to others? He was denying the power of the gods to protect anyone from old age and death?

He was scoffing, or so it seemed, at Brahman? He was deliberately denying the Atman?

Arada was disturbed, but he did not drive the young man away from his ashrama. Instead, he invited Gautama to stay on, to listen, to develop his ideas. "All that I know, you know. The law that I teach, you can expound. Perhaps you have even fathomed points that escape me." There was an anxious silence as Gautama began to speak of pain, to illustrate how everything in creation suffers, and while we may fail to perceive this immediately, it will one day become inescapably manifest. Of course, he could not yet offer a solution to such agonizing problems; indeed, he had come to ask the Brahmans to help him find one.

But what could they do—the famous scholar, or his most perceptive pupils, or the masters drawn to his ashrama from afar by their curiosity to learn the unknown? They led the young man along the byways of truth with brilliant digressions on plurality, on universality, on unity in duality. These are all very pertinent things, agreed, and far from being only lofty ramblings to which the centuries have offered us a key. They taught him the formulas that unite sacrificer and divinity; they revealed the significance of the three key words "*tat tvam asi*," which mean "You [the individual] are that [universal essence]," and through which the human being loses his painful sense of limitation. These eminent men sensed that they had found an equal—if not a brother—in this inspired newcomer and, therefore, they unveiled to him the profoundest meanings of OM, the sacred syllable, and sought to help him understand Brahman, the organizing Word.

One of the masters went on to explain to him that transmigration rewarded or punished every man; that the impalpable force inhabiting a living body would be seen again on earth, elevated to a superior degree if, during his lifetime, the subject had prepared his future with prayers, offerings to the gods, and meditation.

All in vain! Gautama refused everything—shelter, food, the instruction considerately offered, and even the request that he set forth his own ideas during the discussions in the ashrama. He went to bid a respectful farewell to Arada. "Your words, alas, have not touched my heart, for I have not found in them either pity for suffering, or any remedy for its cure. What I seek is the liberation of man, but *you* . . . you do not even care that a man become a better person. You people seek only to be powerful. You care only to enslave the gods."

What a long, deceptive journey it was! One would have thought that his own granitelike character and the obstacles that constantly beset him would somehow guarantee his ultimately reaching his goal. Yet Gautama's every effort was sealed by failure. Every road that he chose came to a dead end. Still he persevered, sustained not by any boundless self-confidence but by some inexplicable certitude.

On his travels, he met another Brahman. It was claimed that wise men came from the ends of the earth to consult this sage, crossing burning deserts, scaling icy mountains, sailing over reaches of water so vast that they voyaged long weeks without sight of land. Some even said that the sage was none other than the incarnation of the divine hero Rama. Entranced by the young man's intelligence, the Brahman, Udraka, soon offered him the direction of his ashrama. More than seven hundred pupils thronged there, most of them of very modest origins and, their master frankly confessed, of very feeble understanding. This was not calculated to discourage Gautama, for he feared nothing so much as excessive formal knowledge and too great facility in assimilation. Yet, one day, he came to the Brahman.

"I am persuaded, venerable master, that the path on which I have embarked with your help will not lead me to indifference to the charms of the world, or to detachment from the passions, or to serenity of spirit. Nor will I find the way to end the vicissitudes of life. . . . And so I must travel further until I find the true path."

This is one of many splendid examples of Brahmanic tolerance and understanding. The deepest differences of opinion do not result in persecution, martydom, or a storm of pamphlets denouncing a heresy. Every man is free to follow his own experience, and it is conceded that he cannot fully communicate its meaning to another. Even today, if a chosen guide is not helpful, the disciple quits him, not ungratefully but with respectful firmness; the master bids the pupil godspeed with kindness and words of hope for the efforts that lie ahead.

And so Guatama left the Brahman Udraka. This time, he was followed by five disciples who sensed, perhaps, that this wise man, still so very young, would reveal to them far more than all the learning and even the experience of an old man. Let us not fail to note their names: they were Kondinya, Ashvajit, Vashpa, Mahanaman, and Bhadrika.

II

FIVE BEAUTIFUL MOUNTAINS ENCIRCLE THE CITY OF RAJAGRIHA, capital of the kingdom of Magadha. Bamboo and palm cluster at their feet; above these tower stands of oak, and higher still rise the blue cedars. Water seeps in dark streaks down the rock faces, collects in small pebbly pools, and flows downward in narrow streams to feed the ponds of Tapovan. These lie under a growth of saplings and tufted reeds, so well concealed that one would never guess water was there if the ear did not detect the splashing of thousands of teal. Two peaks stand guard over this grandiose landscape—Ratnagiri, the Jeweled Mountain, and Sailagiri, Peak of the Vultures. So inaccessible were their upper slopes that no dwelling was ever built there or sheep led there to pasture.

Nor has much changed for almost two thousand and five hundred years, except that, with time, devout followers have cut their way through the dense forest that covers the slopes, and the stones of their path have been worn smooth under the feet of pilgrims come to visit the grotto where Gautama meditated. Still standing below this grotto are groves of mango and jujube trees, then beech, then ilex. As one climbs higher, the rock itself appears, its fissures offering scant hospitality to the wild fig trees that have rooted there.

Actually, it was not a grotto that Gautama lived in. It was merely a craggy recess in the rock, protected by an overhang. A yogi had pointed it out to him, quite likely with the secret notion that fear would push the intimidated neophyte to a show of impudent presumption. Indeed, the roaring of tigers, the screaming of monkeys, the shrieks of hunted wild beasts dying of their wounds in the night, the hissing of the wind, the clapping of the wings of vultures come to verify that the hermit was still there (he their ultimate feast), the hooting of screech owls—all these might well have filled the bravest heart with terror. And in the hot midday when all life, even the insects, was stilled and the forest breathed silence, rending hallucinations were more demoralizing than the darkness fraught with imagined violence.

For weeks and months, Gautama endured torrential rains and torrid heat, icy nights and raging storms. Sometimes he went down as far as the valley to beg a little food, and on his return, had to contend with a pack of jackals for his grass couch, which they had appropriated. He would resume his meditation, as motionless as the rock behind him. He sat so still that a quail flew down to nest between his feet and ring-doves, drawn by his bowl of rice, scattered their droppings on his head; vultures came lurching up and nipped his flesh to make sure that this was no putrefying corpse.

From dawn until deep night he sat plunged in thought,

noticing neither the course of the sun nor the rising of the stars. Then he dozed a little, just so long as the moon takes to run a tenth part of her cloudy way. Roused by the wild cock that crows twice, he arose as the eastern sky was paling, and waited, hands joined palm to palm, to worship the morning star.

This last was a yogi practice, the only one, together with meditation, to which Gautama submitted. The rishis of the forest, who lived in caves below him, inflicted tortures on their bodies that did not seem to him to lead to truth. They crucified flesh and nerves until the sense of pain was destroyed. Some held their arms upraised until these stiffened limbs stuck out like dead branches on a tree. Some had clenched their fists with such ferocious strength that the nails, pressing inward, found their way between the bones and emerged at the back of the hand. Still others walked on sandals studded with sharp nails, or slashed chest and arms with razor-edged stones, or every morning scarified their thighs with embers from their wood fire, or scratched their cheeks, sides, and backs with long thorns torn from the cactus in the valley.

Covered with ashes and mud, desiccated by the weather, mutilated, scurfy, and rheumy-eyed, they applied themselves to senseless occupations. Thousands upon thousands of times they repeated the same prayer or the same holy word, with their eyes closed or fixed on one bright spot, holding their breath until they were overcome by vertigo and, finally, unconsciousness. One counted out a thousand grains of millet and then ate them one by one so as not to satisfy his hunger; another ground his dried peas with bitter and hot leaves so that his palate would be mortified; still another would wander all day long in search of a very rare species of lizard, which he ate raw.

Strange, strange were the roads followed by these men who sought eternal salvation but also longed so desperately to live. Gautama often passed them on his way down to the village, and he was distressed to see them multiply and intensify the hardships of existence. When he remonstrated with them, they answered him proudly: "If a man mortifies his body until the pain grows so intense that he can only hope for the delight and release of death, then his suffering becomes the means whereby he cleanses himself of sin. His purified soul will soar up from the furnace of his affliction toward unimaginable splendor."

"A cloud that is formed by the evaporation of the earth's waters will always fall once more as rain," Gautama objected. "And having returned, the water must again run its muddy course before again it finds the Ganges and is again drawn up by the sun. Your agony of living, were it suspended for thousands of years, must inevitably recommence. And your gods, in whose arms you long to rest—are your gods themselves eternal?"

Disgruntled, the yogis, brahmacharis, and rishis muttered the name of Siva five hundred times, threw mud or ashes on their heads, and cried, "You are only a king's son! Why do you come to annoy us? We have chosen this road, and we will follow it to the end, were all its stones of fire. If you know another way, show it to us. If not, go in peace."

Gautama was far from denying the charm of nature. His disciple and cousin Ananda, who gathered his sayings together, tells us how the Wise One often recalled his arrival in the country of Uruvilva. "It was a delightful corner of the earth. The streams were swift, and I found charming places where I could bathe. Indeed, it seemed to me the most suitable place in which a pure heart might search for the way to salvation."

It is true that one finds a restful contrast between the

steep mountains of Barbar, where the rock rears red from among the tree roots, and the gentle plain across which the Nairanjana and the Mohana flow along their parallel courses. Mango trees, sugar palms, kapok trees, and teak flourish in the sandy soil. Dense forests scale the lower slopes of the mountains; brooks nourish vegetation that even the cruel Indian summer cannot wither. There are numerous hamlets of low houses with thatched roofs and fruit-laden vines. The meanest wall is a thicket abloom with flowers and yellow butterflies; the rippling of the water as it slips through the half-closed gates of the irrigation canals invites the man who is happy and unburdened by problems to sit down and take his ease.

But if Gautama sat down, if he abandoned himself to the sweet refreshment of this countryside, it was the better to reflect on the ways of destiny, on the secrets of the silence out of which all things come, on the secrets of the shadows to which all things return. He saw clearly how the beginning and the end of life were like the abutments of a bridge, and he glimpsed the outline of the arching span that joined them. But as he strove to discern the details, the supports became columns of fog, shelving and shifting at the two ends of a dissolving rainbow. Neither birth nor death delivered up their secret to him, and no more did life.

At first, the young man was robust, and he cared for his health, and went down every day to bathe in the nearby river. He was even mindful of a decent appearance. Noticing that, with time, the hunter's clothing had become more holes than whole cloth, he had picked up from a tomb the linen shroud in which the body of a young slave had been wrapped. He judged he was doing no harm to this recently abandoned husk of humanity by taking something so useless from it. He washed the reddish-yellow linen in the Nairanjana and cut it into pieces out of which he fashioned a robe, a belt, and a scarf.

But every day his thoughts absorbed him more deeply. So deeply that he forgot daily to exercise every muscle, one after the other, as the yogi had taught him. Even the need for food escaped him. Sometimes several days would pass before he noticed that his bowl was empty! And even then he would simply gather up wild fruit that some monkey or parrot had shaken from a tree. On this diet he grew thin, thin, thin. . . . His skin, once white and so smooth against the cheek of Gopa, stuck, dark and leathery, to a skeleton every bone of which it tightly embraced. His ribs flared out above withered thighs. His skull grew to resemble a dried gourd. In his blackened face, his pupils glittered from sunken eye pits like the reflection of stars on the bottom of a well gone nearly dry. The thirty-two signs of beauty faded slowly but irresistibly. No more than a tarnished autumn leaf recalls the tender bud of spring did this scarcely breathing corpse evoke the delicate and handsome Siddhartha of Vishramvan.

Some children had discovered the path to his retreat, and once they had overcome their astonishment at his immobility, they began to treat him with great disrespect, confident that he would not stir. At that age one sees only the ridiculous, feels only revulsion; one does not perceive holiness. They threw goat dung and little stones at him to elicit at least an impatient word. Growing bolder, they touched him, although timidly, or sprinkled dust on his shriveled head. Then they lost interest, like so many crows that have taken the measure of a scarecrow planted in the middle of the field. An elder of the village of Uruvilva came to apologize for them. In the Indian way, he assumed the blame for individuals in the collectivity he administered. "I threw stones at you. But I did not know who you were. I humbly beg your pardon." Gautama did not appear to be aware of his presence.

Some girls came to sneer at him under his very nose, and they also went off, disappointed that the Meditating One had not even opened his eyes to take notice of their youthful taunts. Two of them, however, were moved by admiration and pity, and they resolved to fetch him food every day—boiled rice, sesame seeds, and freshly picked fruit. But how often they found the bowl still full or nibbled at only by some greedy animal! Unnoticed by the anchorite, they sat near him, fanned him, chased gadflies and mosquitoes. Before leaving, they outlined a thick circle of hot coals on the earth so that snakes would not draw near him, and then, at evening, they returned with full hearts to their village of Senani.

It was not that Gautama wished to practice the asceticism of a yogi or brahmachari, or to torture his body to drive out sin. In the beginning, he had simply envisaged reducing the importance of his body so as to strengthen his spirit and free it from the bonds of matter, but his initial intoxicating lucidity gave way to a total obliviousness of his physical self. A dangerous meshing of consequences! What was first an aid to thought became an obstacle. Nature does not allow herself to be violated with impunity; the brain functions only if the body supports and renews its vigor. In modern terms, Gautama was physically overweakened and was succumbing to cerebral anemia.

His five disciples greatly admired him, although they themselves did not feel capable of pursuing so rigorous an experiment. Their Master had not insisted that they share in his struggle with his passions, yet they sensed that he would lead them to some great revelation. And they could not help but be moved to see the Wise One grow, little by little, to look like a mummy. At times, one or another of them had to move very close to him to catch the faint breath escaping from his nostrils.

From the height of the Tushita heaven where she had been welcomed by the gods, Queen Maya became aware of the sad state of her son, her little long-eared elephant. Obeying a mother's impulse, she descended from the empyrean and alighted on the banks of the Nairanjana, moving so swiftly that the Apsarases could scarcely keep up with her. When she saw Siddhartha rigid, dry as a branch in winter, she could not hold back her tears.

"O my son, Asita prophesied that you would reign over the whole world, and here you are, dead, miserable, and alone. Who will call you back to life, my jewel, whom I created from my own body and bore for ten months in my womb?"

But as she was scattering armfuls of flowers over the inert form, Gautama moved, and without opening his eyes, he smiled tenderly.

"Do not be afraid, revered mother. Asita did not lie. Let the earth be split, let Mount Meru sink beneath the waters, let the stars be quenched; I will survive, even if in a ravaged world, and I will bring deliverance to those who are waiting."

Tradition has it that a goatsherd was passing by, leading his beasts. Seeing that Gautama lay prostrate, his breathing inaudible, his lips cracked, and his eyes sunk deep in their pits, he hurried first to gather branches from an apple tree from which he fashioned a leafy shelter. Then he led a goat directly over the Master's head and directed a stream of milk into the half-opened mouth. Such was the marvelous delicacy of a humble man who, being of low caste, feared to touch anything about this man whom he intuitively knew to be noble and holy. And a voice, coming from he knew not where, fell on his ears: "There is no caste, either in the blood that flows, ever the same color, through all veins, or in the tears that fall, salty, from all eyes. No man is born with the red tilka on his forehead and the sacred cord across his chest. Thou hast shared all thou hast with me; when I have achieved the purpose of my search, it will stand thee in good stead."

From that day, Gautama began to recover his strength. The two eldest daughters of the village leader noticed that he had eaten from the bowl of food they still fetched faithfully every evening, and they brought him a big platter of lamb curry. He left the meat untouched but did valiantly by the rest. So, all ten sisters took turns in concocting varied and appetizing menus for him. The Wise One of the forest visibly regained his strength and looks. Soon he resumed his habit of making the rounds of neighboring villages, where the inhabitants vied for the honor of pouring into his bowl the most delicious food they could prepare.

It was, perhaps, a band of bayaderes and musicians who determined the destiny of Gautama—assuming, of course, that all was not willed and directed by the Bodhisattva. Some temple dancers, traveling with their accompanists, had paused at the mouth of a cave during a thunder shower. They were quite incapable of sitting or standing still for long, and they had begun to dance, moving their heads in the precise, brusque motions decreed by tradition, while their arms and hips swayed in sinuous, voluptuous movements. Tiny silver bells strung round their brown ankles played a gay duet with tinkling bracelets on their wrists.

As a musician plucked the copper strings of his cithara, one of the bayaderes sang, laughing and flashing her teeth: "Tune thy cithara, not too high, not too low, and we will cause the gods to be merry, the gods to be merry, and the hearts of men to leap.

"The string that is too tightly drawn must snap, and away the music flies. The string that is too slackly drawn is mute, and so the music dies. Tune thy cithara then, tune thy cithara to the harmonious mean."

It was not the graceful dancer in her swirling skirts or the music that captured Gautama's attention, but rather the words of the frivolous song.

"Fools often teach the wise. . . . Perhaps I have stretched my life string too far, trying to make audible the harmony that will save mankind. My eyes grew weary trying to see the Truth, my strength ran out when I needed it most. I confess my error—an error that I have prolonged for years!"

The five disciples who had left Udraka to accompany him did not hide their disappointment.

"And this is the man who claimed to be teaching us the Truth! His austerities have not led him to acquire enlightenment, so now he dismisses them as useless. This king's son could not dwell on holy works for long. We took him for a wise man. We were wrong. He's nothing but a fool and an ignoramus."

Disdainfully, they spat on the ground and, one after another, like dun-colored ducks filing along the irrigation canals of a rice field, they set out on the road to Benares.

No, the path that leads to deliverance from suffering is not mortification. One further year of reflection and the frequent sight of ascetics (woefully haggard for all the joy in their eyes) definitely turned Gautama away from this hell on earth. The delight of trees that sing with the wind, the beguiling gaiety of bulbul, wood dove, butterfly, and the bee plundering the jasmine, finally persuaded him that nothing in nature mutilates itself in seeking a better way to live.

He was walking down toward Rajagriha one day when a clamorous cloud of dust barred his way. Striding on into the haze, he finally made out a flock of black lambs, a herd of white goats, and one would almost have said a veritable army of men, there were so many excited, shouting shepherds. They were indeed having a hard time to keep their little procession in order; let a tuft of grass or a tempting brook be glimpsed, and off twenty eager animals would trot.

"Where are you taking your flocks? It isn't usual to drive them through the midday heat."

"Our orders are to get one hundred white and one hundred black animals to town in time for the sacrifice that the King must offer tomorrow morning," the shepherds answered, energetically nudging their unruly charges along with their staffs. "We left at dawn, but, even so, we'll scarcely make it by nightfall. We've had to stop every other minute. Look! Just look at that pair! The lamb has hurt itself and the ewe can't decide whether to stay with it or to follow the others. Come on, come on! Let's leave the poor bloody thing here; it will never have the strength to get to town."

But Gautama had already lifted the lamb in his arms; its hoof stained his tunic. He was gently explaining to it: "It's better, isn't it, to carry you and to keep you from suffering than to sit in some cave thinking about the evils of the universe?"

In a hubbub of bleatings and baaings and shouts, the flocks trooped into the outskirts of Rajagriha as the last, low-darting rays of the sun gilded the waters of the Sona. Already great patches of shadow were eating into the streets and squares; the fruit vendors in the bazaar were folding their stalls and, under the lofty gates of the citadel, the guards were preparing to light the black pitch torches. Silence fell over the scene as Gautama appeared in the wake of the flocks, the lamb still in his arms. Wrangling merchants abruptly suspended their exchange of vigorous insults; a blacksmith stood frozen, his hammer raised in the air; the weaver forgot to push his shuttle; by mistake, the scribe put his stylus in his mouth; the money-changer made an error in favor of his client; the white bull of Siva, which was wandering through the streets, ambled into a house and ate the rice that no one remembered to guard; milk spilled from pails left tilted by the milkers. And a humming filled the city, as in an alerted beehive: "Who is this man? How gentle he seems! Is he a god leading animals to his own sacrifice? Look! There's not a speck of dust on his skin!" Then a woman cried: "I know! . . . As I was carrying rice to the rishis on the mountain, I saw, far above them, this saint who was praying for other men."

Bimbisara, King of Magadha, stood erect, facing the altar. Three Brahmans, kneeling until their foreheads touched the floor, were murmuring prayers at incredible speed while monks, wearing white loincloths and the sacred cord across their chests, chanted the mantras of the holocaust. On the altar, which was fashioned of ten thousand and eight hundred bricks—matching in number the pieces into which Purusha had dispersed itself—the fire glowed, springing from fragrant wood, fed by oils, and sprinkled with soma. A trench hollowed from stone guided a stream of thick blood into a trough around which the faithful crowded, dipping three fingers into it and anointing their foreheads and those of their children.

Custom having grown less savage, it was many centuries since prisoners of war had been slaughtered; the gods had had to accept offerings of the blood of animals, the quantity making up for the quality of the victims. No cattle—out of respect for the sacred cow Aditi—but goats, lambs, and cocks.

When Gautama entered, a long-horned goat was stretched out on the altar, its head pulled back by a rope so that its neck hung over the trench. A Brahman was holding a knife to its exposed throat, murmuring, "Here, O Terrible Ones, is the sacrifice that our Sovereign offers. May the sins of the King pass into this animal and may the fire consume them." But at the sound of a loud voice he stayed his hand.

"Do not allow this blow to be struck, great King!"

Taking advantage of the amazement that kept all present rooted to the spot, the new arrival spoke to them. He spoke of the precious life that unites all living creatures; he evoked the trust that animals have put into the hands of the very men who slaughter them; he reminded the Brahmans how, after death, such and such a human being becomes bird or four-footed beast, and that they were, perhaps, cutting the throat of some one of their grandparents.

"Who will believe that spirit can be purified by blood and fire? If the gods are good, who can imagine that blood can delight them, and if they are evil, that sacrifice can bribe them? . . . No, no . . . No man can place on the head of an innocent beast a hair's weight of those misdeeds for which he alone is responsible. I have not studied your books, O Brahmans, but I well know that the universe metes out good for good and evil for evil—and this by strict reckoning. The tree of the future bears the fruit of the past; this you must learn."

Touched to the heart, King Bimbisara, without saying a word, untied the rope that bound the goat, smothered the holy fire, and scattered sand in the blood-red trough. Then, with hands joined and head bowed, he walked three times around the stranger and ended by kneeling and touching his forehead to the feet of Gautama. This humble homage performed, he rose and, more regal than ever, he proclaimed: "Let heralds set forth this day unto the smallest village in my kingdom. This is what they will solemnly announce: 'Hear ye, hear ye, this is the King's will. Henceforth no man shall shed blood for sacrifice. No man shall kill any animal to eat of its flesh. Life is one, and mercy is reserved to the merciful.' "

Because his subjects were so devoted that they came to the palace to report all they knew, Bimbisara presently learned who the surprising stranger was. Accordingly, he sent messengers to search for him—for he had disappeared. He was found, finally, in a forest, absorbed in thought. Without delay, the King put on the robes he wore when receiving a fellow monarch, and accompanied by the humblest groom from his stables, he went, without any royal retinue, to greet Gautama. At that moment the wanderer was eating a bowl of sweet potatoes that a woman of the vicinity, wonder-struck by his beauty, had come, without any disturbing chatter, to lay discreetly at his feet.

"O friend, my joy at seeing thee is great. But thou must no longer lead this ascetic's life. Thy hands are made to hold the reins of empire, not the wooden bowl. Thou art of noble stock, and I propose that thou join together with me in governing my lands. The excellent master is he who possesses at once power, royal wealth, and holiness, he who enjoys his possessions with measure and magnanimity."

"You are my brother in years, and I can talk to you as a brother," the mendicant prince answered. "Your reputation for liberal thinking, for religious feeling, and for prudence has long been great in the country from which I come. But what would I do with wealth? What would I do with power if I cannot subdue old age, sickness, and death? And what would I do were I to speak to you alone words that would soften your heart like the spring rains, when all men are waiting to hear the words that will deliver them . . . words that I will discover only by thinking about them? Go, O King, and understand that loving compassion is the greatest of treasures."

In the month of May every village decked itself out in festive style to honor its local genie. The young girls went to the river for water, which they carried back in hollow bamboo stems; the older women carefully removed the lice from the flowers so that their corollas would be immaculate; the men carted away refuse accumulated over the past twelve months, and whitewashed the houses; the children fetched boughs from the forest to mark out the route for the procession.

In the village of Senani, the wife of its first citizen had been chosen to prepare the consecrated milk, a delicate task quite rightly awarded to this young woman: by her devoutness during the year, Sujata had won the fertility that had until then been denied her by Lakshmi, wife of Vishnu and goddess of prosperity. The preparation of this offering was a complicated operation. It was necessary to feed five hundred cows on the milk of a thousand others; to give the milk of the five hundred to a third group of two hundred, and by successively reducing the number of cows until there were only eight, to obtain a quintessence of milk. To this heavy cream was added sandalwood, spices, and rice selected grain by grain and finely ground, and the whole was brought to a boil. This mixture was then thickened with honey so that when it had cooled, it made a kind of pastry.

This time the caldron began to boil before Sujata had even lighted the fire, and a trickle of fragrant honey formed in the air and fell directly into the cream. The young woman dropped her ladle in amazement.

At that same moment, her slave girl Purna—a scrawny little creature—arrived, all out of breath, her hair all undone, her words tumbling forth like a torrent. "Mistress! . . . Mistress! I was sweeping the ground around the roots of the holy banyan tree for tomorrow's feast when I saw a light. I went over to it, and there I found the genie. He was asleep, but he woke up and smiled at me. He was so handsome! . . . No, no, mistress! I wasn't dreaming! And the proof is, you're going to see him, too. He's following me. Your eyes won't be able to look at him, he's so bright.

The evening before, Gautama had, indeed, fallen asleep between the roots that grew from the low branches of the banyan, fell straight down and implanted themselves in the earth. Here he had dreamed five dreams. The earth was his couch and the Himalayas his pillow. . . . A reed sprang from his navel and its head touched the blue arch of the sky. . . . Whitish worms issued from the earth, and climbing up along his legs, covered his thighs. . . . Birds flew from the eight cardinal points, and dipping down from on high, turned a golden hue as they drew near. . . . He crossed over a mountain of stinking filth without being soiled.

He had been thinking about these curious dreams when little Purna arrived. Seeing that she was frightened, he at once got up. As he passed near the Nairanjana, he paused to bathe, and then took the road leading to Sujata's house. The young woman was not too surprised by the light that suddenly filled her house, for from a genie one may properly expect everything in the way of miracles. Seven times she circled the stranger and then kneeled to wash the dust of the road from his august feet, pouring over them water scented with rose and jasmine.

Then she slipped the ceremonial pastry onto the golden platter her husband had given her for the birth of their child, and covering her head with scarlet silk, she offered it to the miraculous visitor. Serenely he cut the dough, out of which he fashioned forty-nine balls the size of a betel nut, and these he swallowed without taking a single mouthful of water. He knew that the moment had come for him to nourish himself for the great meditation that lay ahead.

Gently he lifted the scarlet veil, and laying his hands on the charming round little head that bowed before him, he said, "May thy happiness be lasting, Sujata! And may the burden of life be light for thy child. . . . But dost thou find, my sister, that life alone is happiness? Is it enough to live and to love?"

Blushing, proud, confused, joyful—all these at once—the young woman, with a flash of pearl-white teeth, smiled at him trustingly. "How could I be anything but happy, with my husband's head on my shoulder and my child's mouth at my breast? For the rest, I believe what the books say. I know that the man who plants a tree, digs a well, and gives a child to his wife, is assured of happiness after death. I believe that good comes from good and that evil begets evil. But if death called my husband before me, I would climb the funeral pyre with joy, for it is said that by doing this a woman wins for her life's companion a million years in the paradise of Indra. For the rest, I try to do what seems to me good, in the hope that what must happen will be good, too."

Pensively, Gautama studied the beautiful, velvety eyes, the plaited hair from which peeped two sprays of jasmine, and the face ennobled by kindness.

"Thou canst teach the teachers, thy simplicity surpasses their knowledge. Be happy that thou art ignorant enough to know the path of justice and duty, O little dove whom the dawn will always return to its nest. Thou hast seen that man is right to hope, thou hast divined that the wheel of life depends on our own actions. May I finish my work as well as thou hast accepted thine own, and so free thee of pain, illness, old age, and death. He whom thou hast taken for a god begs you to pray for this wish."

Without waiting for an answer, he walked away, carrying with him the now empty golden platter, which Sujata had laughingly begged him to take: "I would be a poor thing, would I not, if I gave the food without the plate!"

Deeply stirred, Gautama strode along the river bank. His whole being trembled with joy, like the heart of a young man at the dawn of his wedding day. Had he really finished with the years of searching, of senseless exercises, of meditations in which thoughts whirl about yet never find a fixed point on which to settle? Skimming the platter far out over the Nairanjana, he cried, "If I am to be enlightened, let this platter float upstream against the current! If not, it will be a sign that I must still look for my path."

Like a quoit the golden disk ricocheted over the water, slowed, and wavered. Gautama's heart thumped as he watched for destiny to make a sign. . . . Then, miraculously, the platter turned, and with steadily mounting speed, swept upstream. In this fashion, it covered more than three hundred arm lengths, tipped up on its rim, balanced a moment to reflect the sun's rays, then sank below the surface of the waters. There was a long pause, and then came two tinkling sounds. Knowing all that we know today, we can state that the platter had fallen through a deep hole in the bed of the stream, down to the shadowy domain of Kala, and at the end of its fall, had knocked against two other platters that, in the very same manner and at the very same place, in preceding cycles of the universe, the two earlier Buddhas who had come down to earth had hurled against the current of the Nairanjana.

Now the Wise One walked confidently toward a fig tree. Day was drawing to a close. Dusk was drowning the earth in shadow, the flowers were folding their petals, the birds were twittering their last calls before the fall of night. The evening air, compounded of the fragrance of fresh-cut grasses, the smoke from hearthfires, and the still warm earth, filled the heart with mildness.

Other flowers were coming into bloom—corollas of jewels tossed down by the gods. Other songs than those of the orioles and warblers sounded—the melodies of lutes strummed by the Gandharvas in the clouds. The rough stones along Gautama's path were transformed into golden sands. Palm trees sprang up as he passed and as quickly disappeared behind him. The rim of the forest sparkled with the thousands of eyes that were following his steps—the eyes of leopards and deer, of screech owls and ringdoves, of serpents and field mice, of frogs and butterflies, all united in peace. Each pool, each pond was covered with lotus flowers that, strange to behold, opened their petals wide as the sun sank and the brilliant clouds paled to a gray-blue.

A reaper returning late from the fields saw Gautama hesitate to sit down. The man tore eight huge handfuls of kusha grass from a haystack and arranged it at the foot of the fig tree; then, slinging his scythe over his shoulder, he went off toward the village, singing.

Seven times Gautama circled the tree, bowing to it, his hands joined. He sat down, facing first the south, then the north, then the west, each time moving the pillow of grass. And each time the earth seemed to tip under his footstep, the horizon sinking lower than the lowest circle of hell. But when the Wise One took his place facing the east, the grass swelled and became the cushion of the throne that suddenly appeared, a cushion softer than a fledgling's down.

Then Gautama crossed his legs, so that each foot rested under the opposite thigh. He closed his eyes, and in a firm voice, he pronounced an oath that the gods, the trees, the birds, and the earth could call to witness. "Let my skin wither, let my hand waste away, let my bones crumble, but until I have gained Supreme Enlightenment, I will not stir from this spot."

Every living thing fell silent, every breath was stayed. The world began an anxious vigil.

Book Five

I

THE EARTH WAS SHROUDED IN DARKNESS BUT A GLORIOUS LIGHT reigned in heaven. The gods were celebrating because the hour of the fourth Buddha, Gautama's hour, had finally come. Indra was blowing on a conch one hundred cubits long, holding each note a longish time; each sound, in fact, lasted the equivalent of four of our human months. Maha Kala was reciting an ode of one hundred thousand strophes. Brahma sat erect on his goose-shaped throne, holding his white parasol high above his head.

With his tongue pressed against his palate, Gautama was driving, goading his mind to the most intense concentration. As an old account puts it, "His red blood had dried up, his bile had dried up, and his saliva likewise."

The body of the Meditating One glowed with a gentle light that penetrated to the kingdom of Mara, god of sensual pleasures, of desire, of attachment to all that man seeks and despairs of not possessing or of losing—in a word, of hell. Mara is not to be confused with the Devil, who receives the sinful souls that Death delivers over to him. Nor with the beguiling and proud fallen Lucifer, nor Ashtoreth, nor Beelzebub. Rather, he is the Enemy, "he who opposes," the Satan presented to us by the Old Testament, the Shadow of God ordered to test the faith of Job. In any case, assuredly Mara was the Evil One.

To his sons and servants who were alarmed by his sudden anxiety, he said, "I do not know if I have been dreaming or if I have had a true vision of the future, but I saw my kingdom darkened by a cloud of dust. My gardens had lost their flowers and leaves, and the fruit lay rotten on the earth. My swans searched in vain for water in the pools, my peacocks had been stripped of their long fantails and slunk in shame to cover. My queen was overcome by remorse and was tearing her hair—gray hair!—and my daughters were dressed in rags that revealed how their bodies had grown faded and repulsive. And you, Sarthavaha—you, my son!—were bowing before some man under a fig tree. I myself was so weak that I could not draw my sword from its scabbard, and I was weeping tears of blood as I watched my palace crumble to the ground."

The sight of his numerous troops restored Mara's courage. Had he not in hand the means with which to vanquish the most potent hero that ever was? Ignoring his son, who had a taste for metaphysics and was trying to expound the notion that the sun alone could make the shining worm seem dull, he mobilized the demons that knew best how to combat wisdom and light: the passions, ignorance, error, lust, greed, obscurantism, malice. Artists have portrayed them for us as Gautama must actually have seen them—horrible creatures, with black, red, or dark-blue faces, flaming eyes, cracked, snarling lips, the ears of pigs, goats, or rabbits; each had a thousand feet and hands, and several heads, and wore ornaments decorated with skulls and serpents. Their weapons they carried concealed in bouquets of flowers.

The demon troops were led by Attavada, or Egoism, who held before him a mirror into which he gazed, murmuring "I . . . I . . . I . . ." To seduce the Buddha, he ordered his warriors to shout, in a chorus of adulation, "Thou, thou art the Mighty One, who judgest the world from the height of thy grandeur!" To the Meditating One, Egoism whispered, "Leave all others and go. . . . Go find rest in thine own eternal light." Egoism was leaning on the arm of pallid Doubt, who hissed ironically, "Vain is the knowledge that seeks to show the vanity of illusion." And he bent down to whisper, "And what if knowledge were only appearance?" He turned, for confirmation, to Scruple, who promptly insinuated, "Dost dare believe thyself wiser than those who wrote the Vedas?"

Crowding behind these figures came Silabbat, the sorceress who dupes the souls of men; Visikitcha, or masked Error; Patigha, or Hatred, who has snakes for hair; Rupagara the lustful; Arunaya, glorifier of strife; the proud, disdainful Mano; Udatcha, or tender and sensitive Self-Love; and that fearsome shrew Avidya, mother of Fear and Injustice; and many, many more!

The last battalion was commanded by the most dangerous leader of all—Kama, lord of the passions, whose power prevailed even among the gods. His golden bow was garlanded with red flowers; thus armed, he played with the arrows of desire, whose five fiery-forked darts cruelly ripped the heart as they were wrenched from it. His troops comprised adorable, languidly dancing female demons. In a lascivious swirling motion, their gowns parted, like petals unfolding to reveal the heart of the flower, and disclosed the two rubies of their breasts. They sang with shameless abandon of the hot desires of their flesh, the sweetness of their embrace, and the perfume of their mouths. Each offered herself, in turn, to the motionless figure, murmuring, "Thou hast known pleasure but never such ecstasy as thou wilt find in my love."

But the Meditating One forced his mind to remain clear and steady: "There is only one love, the love for all men," and the figures dissolved into a light fog that was dispersed by the breeze.

Before launching his own attack, Mara was eager to wear down his enemy's powers of resistance. Gautama was, after all, only a mortal man; it was possible to break his nerve. Accordingly, the Evil One unleashed the fury of the winds. From the full circle of the horizon furious storms broke forth. In their irresistible onward rush they shook mountains; tossed whole forests into lakes, like so many straws; drove flowing rivers back upon themselves to their sources; ripped off the roofs of houses, and upturned the very soil of the fields. Not a fold of the robe of Gautama stirred.

"You see?" said Sarthavaha. "You think he's a coward because he is calm. You don't know his strength."

Whereupon Mara summoned the rains. To the crashing of thunder, they flooded the earth. The gods had taken refuge behind the clouds, and only their anxious eyes were visible. The waters rose to the treetops, covered whole villages, turned what had been a smiling countryside into a turbulent ocean. Not a drop of water stained the scarf of Gautama.

"Did you hear what he said? 'If I truly possess the ten perfect virtues, I shall be able to prevail!' "

"He does not possess them!" roared Mara. "And even if he did . . ."

This time flaming stones, from sharp-honed flints to heavy slabs of granite, fell from the heavens. In a luminous trail these projectiles streaked across the night sky, but as they approached the fig tree they turned into fragrant roses. As red-hot cinders touched the earth they formed a carpet of sandalwood powder and the very mud was transformed into a perfumed oil that protected Gautama.

Sarthavaha saw his father glancing about him, ready to order the final assault, and he shouted again, "You're mad! Even if you were equal in number to the sands of the Ganges, you would not move a hair of his head! And you think you are capable of killing him? It will be he, he, *he*, through his wisdom, who will conquer you."

But a thick cloud of arrows was already buzzing overhead, like an angry swarm of bees, and fell to blanket the earth with anemones. Javelins soared aloft in a hissing arc and floated down like a myriad lilies; double-edged axes hurtled through the air with a terrifying roar and fell lightly to the ground, garlanded with fragrant woodbine. Then Mara hurled his razor-edged discus, a weapon that never missed its mark. With a whirl of sparks the disk circled Gautama, hung poised for an instant over his head, like a cloud, and boomeranged on the stupefied demons. Mara stamped with rage and screamed, "Impostor! You sit in a seat that is not yours! Until a Bodhisattva has won the right to sit there because of his ten perfections, he belongs to me. . . . What merits can you claim? Show me one witness to your liberality, and I will concede your right to this throne. I can show you proofs of my liberality by the thousands. How can these cowards who have given up the fight refuse to admit what they owe me!"

A Hurvari backed up this challenge. "I will testify, Mara! I will testify. You have done more for me than Brahma himself could have done, if he had deigned to concern himself with me or my desires!"

"You hear? You hear that? Now, you produce one single witness!"

Gautama opened his eyes, and looking at Mara with great gentleness, he dropped his right hand. "Of course you have witnesses. But do they not come from among the living, from creatures who are blindly devoted to you because of the fleeting pleasures you have prodigally showered on them? My witnesses? I have none."

A murmur of satisfaction spread among Mara's partisans.

"No, I have no one. . . . But Earth will bear witness, although it has never profited thereby, that in the past I have shown my generosity more than seven hundred times. I tell you this world belongs to me—and you are the last who can challenge my sovereignty."

As he spoke, Gautama touched the earth with three fingers of his right hand, as much to call it to witness as to affirm his possession of it.

And a grave voice rose from the soil. "Yes, I who am the Earth, Mother of all creatures, I can bear witness to his generosity. . . . A thousand times, a hundred thousand times, in the course of previous existences, he has given his eyes, his hands, his body, his heart. Without hesitation, without stint, gladly . . . Retreat, Mara, for in generosity as in strength he has vanquished you."

During the first vigil of the night, Gautama saw once again his five hundred and fifty previous lives. He was like a traveler who, from the summit he has painfully reached, looks back over the road he has covered. He sees the broad highways; the twisting mountain trails where he nearly lost his footing; the ravines; the pathless forests; the precipices he skirted; the marshes where he risked losing his way; the quagmires that lay waiting for him to sink down exhausted; the mirages that he had too often taken for the lofty goal he was seeking; the cataracts and the swamps; the friendly villages and those that had turned him out; the plains where, from a distance, life looked deceptively easy; and the heights on which man gives the best of himself as he scales them. On that long journey, no step had been taken that did not follow from the preceding step and direct the next one; each failure had resulted from error; each happy progression had harvested earlier efforts, preserving the profit earned and standing as pledge against its possible loss.

Although he had never studied the sticks the peasants used to notch or examined the ledgers of merchants, Gautama conceived of debit and credit, of asset and liability. Death halts the entries; the columns are totaled, the page is turned, and the balance of merits and demerits is carried forward, accurately and fairly, to the head of a fresh page for a new life that begins lightened or burdened thereby.

His second vigil revealed to the Meditating One the state of the universe. Soberly and serenely, he contemplated the earth, the satellites, the suns, the stars living and dead, the stellar systems, and the nebulae which move with marvelous regularity, subordinating their independence to a perfect balance between the forces of attraction and repulsion. Suddenly he perceived the whole of revolving time, the numberless days of Brahma—each equivalent to four billion, three hundred and twenty million human years—in the course of which worlds appear, grow, stabilize, and disappear.

And he saw how, through era after era, the unvarying, silent Law persists, demanding that darkness evolve into light and death into life, giving form to what was only promise or possibility, governing an order that no man built or has ever denied. A nameless, formless Power of unimaginable potency exists, which is superior to the gods; ineffable, unchangeable, and sovereign, it governs all. Whatever submits to it is good, whatever seeks to oppose it is evil.

In the course of his third vigil, Gautama conceded the utility, in the universal order, of the worm, of the tiger, and of the butterfly. He came to see that the kite which, to feed its young, murders the field mouse is not to be condemned any more than is the hungry field mouse condemned for nibbling the pears on the tree. Everything, he saw, is indispensable to life—the drop of dew and the star, the shrimp and the acorn, the elephant and the river—from the moment that each thing acts in conformity to its own nature.

Man himself, if he lives his life so as to die well, if he has undertaken to help other creatures, all of whom also suffer from the miseries of existence, dies with hopeful prospects for his ultimate salvation. This insight prepared Gautama for the discoveries of his last vigil.

In this final vision of the night, the Four Noble Truths were revealed, one by one. Does suffering not hang like a pall over life, and does it not cease when life ceases? Suffering enters the world in the umbilical cord of the infant; it crouches within man's being and assails him when he least expects it, and is given up only with life itself. No one can hope to escape its hold unless he learns its nature and cause, unless he banishes false ideas and acquires, instead, a true view of it.

How pitiable is the state of the man who does not see that illusion engenders perverse impulses and fosters a disastrous energy in the envelope that is the physical body. With his eyes, ears, his very skin and nerves defenselessly exposed to sensation, man is a mirror reflecting only appearances. Fortified by false joys and sorrows, the life of the senses burgeons, yet it is consumed by thirst. For Trishna, or Desire, never quenches thirst but maliciously whets it with pleasure, glory, ambition, love, pride, avarice, luxury—all draughts as thirst-quenching as is salt water. They imperiously demand more, more, more, and yet more.

If desire is uprooted from the soul of the wise man, if illusion is banished and if his senses are mastered; if his spirit is freed of all possessive attachments and the drive toward conquest and revenge is rooted out—if all this has been achieved, then the passions will die of hunger. Gautama saw this, yet one problem still confronted him: suppose a man's life is unshackled from the chains of desire. Would not illness, old age, and death—the undeniable sources of pain—still make him suffer? And even if a man endured these agonies with a serene heart, would he not encounter them again in yet another existence? "What a wretched world it is! It grows old and dies, and it is reborn to grown old and to die again, forever plunged in suffering! And this without end?"

Fired by an implacable logic, the Meditating One worked back, link by link, along the chain of causality:

Old age and death would not exist were it not for birth;
The cause of birth is the life that engenders it;
Life is perpetuated because there is attachment;
Attachment is created by craving;
Craving is engendered by sensation;
There is no craving without contact;
There is no contact without the intervention of the senses;
The senses account for name and form;
Name and form exist because there is consciousness;
There is no consciousness without perception;
The sole cause of perception is ignorance, which creates and deforms it, and abandons man to its mercy.

Thus, moving from cause to cause, the Meditating One reached the origin of the implacable chain. And then the ultimate Truth flashed forth: "By dissipating ignorance, by killing desire, which leads from birth to birth in the search for satiety, the desire for rebirth will disappear of itself since it will have no object. Then there will be no more occasion for suffering."

Beyond any doubt, the solution for man lay here—to live no longer! This did not mean that he should voluntarily subject himself to premature death, for suicide does not belie a wish to throw the dice once more, to try for a new and better life. It meant that a man must realize fully that the lures on which he bases his joy at being on this earth are false and futile.

With unsparing clarity Gautama now saw the way offered the wise man is this: he must be master of himself; he must acquire the Enlightenment that enables him to assess illusion; he must free himself of all desire. The karma of such a man—that is, the sum of all his earlier thoughts and deeds—would stand him in good stead in the transmigrations still to come. For certainly he would still need many lives—thousands of them, perhaps—each of which would be increasingly cleansed of pride, ignorance, and desire. But eventually the wise one would enter new forms and would experience less and less suffering.

Delivered from error, he would no longer be the slave of the skandhas, the five basic elements of man's constitution, all of which are impermanent. He would no longer attribute constancy to his body, feelings, perceptions, impulses, emotions, or consciousness.

Finally, at the end of less and less burdensome births, there would be no further need for the karma to return to find a body and a place for rebirth; it would have reached the end of the path.

And this arrival at the end of the road? Once so remote and now so accessible, what exactly was it? An impasse, a triumph? . . . The reply came to him in a blinding flash: The Wheel of Life, the wheel of eternal rebirths in one of the six worlds, would no longer have to turn. A new kind of existence would begin for this enlightened man—not dissolution, not nothingness. It would not even be life as we understand that. It would be the peaceful cessation of the obligation to be reborn; it would be definitive repose in the realm of non-being —or of no-longer-being—that never changes.

The fourth vigil was drawing to a close. In his twofold contemplation of the chain of causation, Gautama had perceived how birth is the cause of death; following the chain back to ignorance, he found that the destruction of ignorance will eliminate birth and, by extension, all suffering. And the Wise One mapped out this road that leads straight and clear to the extinction of suffering, and he called it the Noble Eightfold Path. Man must possess right understanding, sincere speech, pure thoughts, and peace of spirit. He must love all that lives. He must turn away from greed and anger to give himself to meditation.

The Enlightened One, the Illumined One—the Buddha, in a word—gave a deep sigh and he turned with delight to the vision of his Bodhisattva Avalokiteshvara, who had given his own strength and compassion to Gautama so that he might become incarnate on earth.

The curtains of night were tinged with a pale mauve, then rose. A warm breeze flowed over the plain of Uruvilva, and the forest awoke to a soft stirring. Soon gold edged the lingering clouds, and the mountains emerged in sharp outline against a brightening sky. The dew on the meadows became a sparkling carpet; the Nairanjana drifted rubies, then circles of molten gold.

The songs of birds, reedlike, cooing, harsh, twittering or trilled in full-throated triumph, called the Illumined One back from his long journey. As the sun sprang up from the horizon, the Buddha cried, "All my life I have searched in vain for the builder of the house. And now thou art discovered—and thou dost build of clouds and on foundations of illusion! But the walls have fallen, the roof has collapsed, and never again wilt thou build. The spirit can achieve Nirvana! Death-bringing birth is no more, for desire is crushed!"

Twelve times the earth trembled for joy. Evil hearts became good, and hearts already kind felt themselves grow better. The assassin dropped his weapon, the thief abandoned his booty, the moneychanger gave a fair rate, the husband became more gentle, children obeyed their parents. Hens pecked between the paws of the fox; together the spotted deer and the tigress nursing her cubs drank at the river's edge. The kite carried twigs to the nest of the finch. Kings warring with each other exchanged gifts and homage; the dying sat laughing on the edge of their deathbeds.

In the sky, the thirty-three gods repeated the triumphal chant of Indra. "He has come, he who will enlighten the world, he who will protect the world. Long blinded, the eye of the world has opened and is drunk with light. O conqueror of all darkness, thou wilt restore all creatures! Guided by thy sublime Law, they will reach the bank of salvation. Thou holdest the lamp, Tathagata! Banish the shadows!"

Sitting by Siddhartha's empty bed, the grieving Gopa Yasodhara felt a sudden joy flood her heart. She knew that her love could not mislead her and that her great sorrow would, in time, be assuaged and transformed into unending joy.

II

DURING THE NIGHT THE THICK GROWTH OF HAIR BETWEEN THE eyebrows of the Buddha was transformed into a silvery wool-like tuft. This was the *urna*, one of the thirty-two signs of beauty that mark an Enlightened One and that would hence-forth distinguish the Buddha from other men. Legend has it that in the late morning, when the sun was growing hot, snails climbed up his body and, with their moist shells, fashioned a fresh helmet to protect him from the burning rays.

The Dhyani Buddhas, who meditate at the cardinal points, dispatched their glorious reflections down to earth. These great kings swooped down from the highest heavens like fal-cons, each bearing a bowl of rice that had been gathered from the far reaches of the world. From the north winged Genii arrived, from the south came corpulent servants armed with parasols and fly-flaps. The Gandharvas traveled from the east, playing the while on their instruments, and emerging from the waters to the west, the Nagas coiled and uncoiled themselves swiftly in the direction of the sacred fig tree. Because they felt ashamed to be bearers of poison, they proposed to offer the most humble homage; lifting their swollen throats, each set with a large ruby, they would hold the bowl in which the rice from the four corners of the earth would be mixed.

For seven weeks the Buddha was to meditate, open-eyed, on his mission. Adamantine, he sat without stirring, his legs crossed under him, and savored the joy of having achieved Enlightenment. "I am delivered!" he thought exultingly, but he was preoccupied to find a way to communicate his knowledge to others.

"What I have done and achieved means, I believe, that I have been beyond all human law. But the knowledge I have acquired is not yet the way of wisdom. It could not put an end to old age, sickness, and death.

"Nothing endures—that is what my brothers must understand. Perishable is the vase of unbaked clay that shatters at the smallest shock. Unstable is the fortune that is lent and that must, one day, be repaid; it is a castle of sand built on shifting sand.

"Everything is in turn both cause and effect; the one is contained within the other as birth is latent in the seed, although the seed is not the semen. Substance, ephemeral as it may be, nonetheless knows no interruption; no thing exists that has not some other thing as its origin; nothing vanishes without first creating. That is the only permanence there is.

"Thus, from cause to effect and from that effect to new effect all syntheses are born. Yet in thinking about these fusions, I have come to see that they are merely a nothingness, a void, and that the void alone is unchangeable. All beings are empty, within and without; no one of them possesses the fixedness that is the true sign of the Law.

"But how can I make my brothers understand the errors that dominate the world and afflict it so grievously?"

Was it not perhaps more worth while, the Buddha asked himself, for him to attain Nirvana immediately? His uncertainty distressed Brahma, and it did not escape the tireless Mara, who was constantly on the alert for any sign of weakening. Now he promptly reappeared.

"O Happy One, you now know the path of deliverance. Why delay? Blow on the lamp, let its flame go out. Your time has come."

The Perfect One was considering how he might win followers for his Law—disciples who, in their turn, would teach the Law to the faithful. Mara signaled to his three daughters to approach the Buddha. They assumed a decent, modest air, the better to disarm the enemy, and they sang sweetly, yet through the poetry flowed all the seductive sensuality that has intoxicated India throughout time.

"Spring draws to a close, sweet friend, and summer, most opulent of seasons, draws near. The trees blossom and their fragrance gladdens our hearts. . . . And thy eyes, sweet lord, shine with a light that stirs our senses. . . . Look upon us. Are we not fashioned to give pleasure to men and to gods?

"Look upon our hair; breathe the jasmine that perfumes it. What pleases thee more—hair yellow as the field of grain, red as beaten leather, or black as the fur of the otter? . . . Choose . . . or take all. Look into our eyes and see the dawn of love. What would delight thee—the pale periwinkle, the green chalcedony, or the warm hazelnut of autumn? . . . Look upon our lips, like fruit the sun has ripened to melting softness. Look upon our breasts, high and firm, burning yet cool, rounded, perfect goblets offering thee a ruby wine. Look upon the curving grace of our hips, the swelling fullness of our thighs, supple as the trunk of the elephant.

"Like swans we move, shoulders smoothly sloping, heads high. We will sing thee songs thou dost love and others thou knowest not. We will dance for thee dances that are chaste yet draw thee close to our bodies. Come, and on the lush tender grass of the meadow, on the marvelous carpets of moss in the forest, come, give thyself to pleasure. . . . Ah! Only a fool scorns such treasure. Look upon us, lord. Choose . . . or take all. Look upon us."

And the Blessed One did indeed look upon them. But so severe was his glance that the seductive girls were instantly withered; their hair thinned, their complexion clouded, their eyes filmed, their lips cracked, and their breasts grew flabby. A shriek of despair split the air from Tibet to Cape Comorin. Like a bemired old elephant, Mara stared stupidly at the disaster.

"Oh, Father! Cure us of this blight of age, give us back our youth and beauty."

"Alas, my poor children, only the Buddha can undo what the Buddha has done. You have been fools. You have been blinded by easy conquests. Do you at least know enough now to feel guilty? . . . Well, then, open your hearts and repent sincerely that you have mistaken so august a character. Perhaps the Merciful One will restore your beauty."

More truly contrite than hopeful, the three little old crones, all tremulous, fell to their knees. They were able not to bemoan their cloud-spun hair, their wide-set eyes, their crimson lips and faultless throats, and to be dismayed only at having offended him who knew all things.

"Yes, fools you have been!" the Tathagata said. "You thought to overturn a mountain by scratching at its base with your nails, to sever an iron bar with your teeth. But you are not completely bereft of good sense since you suffer now for your mistake. So, young women, you are forgiven. And while waiting for the ever near and painful true old age, may each of you become the happiness of one man—her husband."

Without stirring from his throne, the Buddha completed a week-long journey in which he traveled through all existing worlds, and this provided food for a week of meditation. The fourth week he spent visiting India, from the Himalayas to the southernmost tip of the peninsula, from the deserts of the Indus to the mouths of the Ganges.

The fifth week was spent in motionless reflection, as he sought to put order in impressions culled from so many travels. But the monsoon season had come, and the rain fell from the skies in cataracts; glacial windstorms swept over the peninsula, and heavy clouds hid the blue heaven. The Nairanjana overflowed its banks and inundated the meadows, threatening the noble throne as well. Mucilinda, king of the Nagas, crept over to the fig tree and, slipping under the seat, raised the throne by the full height of the seven rings in which he had coiled himself. Spreading the seven heads that grew from his single, enormous throat, he formed a kind of hollowed shell behind the Buddha's head to protect him. When the storms subsided, Mucilinda uncurled and assumed the figure of a handsome young man worshiping the Blessed One.

During the sixth week, the Perfect One conversed with the gods, who had come down to earth to greet him. And the last week of the Illumination was spent in a searching discussion with Brahma. "Until now," the first among the gods said, "an evil law has obtained, and it has led mankind into the ways of sinfulness. Look upon the wretched races of humanity, O Saviour, and be thou their guide and their light. Speak, teach. . . . There will be many who will understand thy message."

The Happy One shook his head. "The Law that I have established is truly profound. It is subtle and hard to comprehend, and lies beyond the grasp of the ordinary man. The world will scoff at it. A few wise men, perhaps, will fathom the meaning of the Law and resolve to submit to it. But if I go out into the world, if I talk to those who do not understand, I will be risking the worst possible defeat."

But Brahma, whose right shoulder is bare in token of submissiveness, kept urging the Happy One.

"Among the lotuses in the pool, some blue, some white or pink, there are those that flourish below the water, while others flower on the surface, and others still grow so high that their blossoms are not even wet. Do you not look at the lotus that opens below the water as well as at the one blooming gloriously in the sun? I am imploring you to accept your mission, and all the gods pray with me that you will."

Before the Buddha had time to reply Mara played his last card. "This hope of thine is doomed," he whispered. "Thou wilt face all the countless creatures who are blind— and who have no wish to be otherwise. Thou wilt be opposed by evil men to whose interest it is that evil and error continue to flourish on earth."

In the heaven of the Thirty-three, Indra felt his throne grow hot like glowing embers, a sign that mankind was being gravely threatened. In less time than a man takes to flex his arm, he descended to intervene. And so it happened that the Buddha at last surrendered to his love for mankind. Deferring his own entrance into Nirvana, he decided to remain on earth to teach others the way to salvation.

"I was thinking of the weary travail that lies ahead, and I was afraid that it would be all in vain. . . . But compassion must guide me. So be it! I am ready, Brahma. For the sake of all those who drift, uncertain and without direction in this world, I will teach the Law."

III

FOR THE FIRST TIME IN FORTY-NINE DAYS, THE INVISIBLE CUR-
tain that concealed the fig tree from the eyes of the citizens of
Uruvilva was lifted. At that moment, two merchants were
passing along the road on their way to Gaya; they were
brothers, Trapusha and Bhallika by name. When they drew
abreast of the fig tree, their wagons suddenly stopped and
neither shouts nor blows could induce the oxen to stir by so
much as a wheel's turn. Catching sight of a poor man seated
under a tree, the brothers went over to ask his help.

As they came nearer, they noticed that a diffused glow
seemed to emanate from the beggar, and half-amused, half-
impressed, they asked each other, "Could this be the genie of

the river? A mountain divinity? Or Brahma himself, maybe?" But when they observed the man's clothes, they concluded that he was some monk begging for his food.

Being devout and eager to insure the safety of their souls by good deeds, the merchants rummaged in their cart for some honey and rice cakes, which they offered the Perfect One. The latter gestured to them that he could receive nothing directly in his hand. Now full of respect, they returned to their wagon for a gold platter on which to present their food. The Buddha indicated that the smallest charity should be offered not on a platter of pure gold but from a pure heart. A little discouraged, the merchants set their little cakes down in a crack in the stone.

"Accept them, holy one. Accept them and be merciful to us."

In their hearts, they heard a voice admonishing them, "He whom you see has attained Enlightenment. The first meal that he will have taken since discovering the way to deliverance he will receive from you, merchants, to whom he has reserved the privilege of offering it. He is about to go out into the world to teach the Law, but you will be the first among men to declare faith in the Buddha."

"From this day forward, may the Blessed One accept us as disciples for so long as we live, for we have put our faith in him."

In token of his acceptance, the Perfect One pulled several hairs from his head, which he gave to the two men. Filled with happiness, the merchants placed them in a leather pouch for safekeeping. A stupa three times seven arm lengths in height was eventually built to house these sacred relics, which were objects of veneration for generations to come.

Trapusha and Bhallika had entrusted themselves in perfect faith to the Buddha, but they did not receive any in-

struction. It was not that the Perfect One did not esteem them
—for him all men were equal—but he wanted the first man to
whom he communicated his message of salvation to have a
heart free of hatred and prejudice, greed and carnal desires.
The man should, furthermore, be intelligent enough to understand more than mere words and active enough not to treat
the revelation as an inviolable secret.

For these reasons, the Perfect One bethought himself of
the Brahman Arada, who would certainly rejoice to spread
the new wisdom. But his mind informed him that the
Brahman had died shortly before. "What a grievous loss for
him, that he died before he heard my Law!" . . . In the same
way, he knew that Udraka, son of Rama, had also departed
from the earth. "What a pity! He, too, would have understood my Law." The Buddha's mind then turned to the five
disciples who had followed him during the years when he was
seeking truth through sterile asceticism. He *saw* that they
were living in a hut which they had built in Rishipatana, in
the Deer Park, on the outskirts of Benares. Accordingly, he
decided to go to Benares without delay and to instruct them.

He made the trip alone, charting the way by his star
Pushya, and sleeping in the forests. The distance was great—
nearly two hundred of our modern miles—but since it was the
month of June and the weather was fine, he was able to cover
long stretches of the road at a time. As he traveled, he girded
himself for the battle he would soon have to fight in the holy
city of a hundred temples. At the ford on the Son, near
Nasriga, he met a monk by the name of Upaka. The man did
not hide his admiration for the transparent beauty that shone
in the Buddha's face. "Ripe fruit is less radiant than thou. If
thou art a religious, dare I inquire who is thy master? Or art
thou the apparition of a jina?"

The Buddha answered simply, "I have had no master.
There is no one who is my equal. I alone am wise, serene of

heart, and free of all corruption. I am the only master in this world, and among the gods, as among men, I am without peer. Yes, thou art right, I am an arhat and jina."

When he reached the south bank of the Ganges, he beckoned to the ferryman. The boatman asked him, as he asked every passenger, for his fare before they embarked. With a smile, the Blessed One remarked that, being a monk, he had not a penny to his name. "No money, no boat," retorted the man. And he nearly fell over when he saw the Blessed One rise in the air, float across the river, and land on the farther bank.

"Woe, woe is me who have refused such a small service to so holy a man!"

From afar the five disciples saw their former forest companion arriving. They followed his approach with a certain surprise and curiosity, and could not resist rather ironic comment.

"Well, here is the famous ascetic who claimed he would find a cure for suffering! At least he's recovered his own health and good looks, hasn't he? He glitters like gold." . . . "Maybe he will want to tell us about his discoveries. Well, we will listen to him, won't we?" . . . "No matter what, we are obliged to make room for him and even to share what little food we have with him. But it will be no pleasure; indeed, no pleasure at all."

As he drew near they began, in a most condescending way, to call him "dear sir"—a form then used only in addressing a connection of lower rank. But as he sat down among them, they felt their hearts soften. Presently they were all aflutter, like birds in a cage under which a fire has been lighted. And it was much worse when he said to them, "I am the Holy One, the Perfect One, the Supreme Buddha. Open thy ears, O monks. The Way has been found. Listen to me."

The words were not boastful; they stated a fact. The Buddha sensed that the disciples were still agitated by some doubt, and he added, "You do recognize, monks, that I never spoke to you like this before?"

Prostrate before a light they felt far more potent than any of the gods they had until then revered, the five monks listened—not so much with their ears as with a sixth sense that was awakening in them.

For a long time the Buddha spoke. The sun was high in its course when he began. The full moon reached its zenith, and it seemed to him that he had not yet said anything essential. When dawn paled the eastern sky, he had not finished. His words pierced the monks like arrows but caused them no pain, only joy. As the sky lightened, several gazelles drew near, charmed, and they also listened to the marvelous sermon and now and then with their fresh, moist noses they nuzzled the Saint's cheek.

"O monks! learn that all existence is nothing but pain. Birth is painful, old age is painful. Death is the supreme pain, because it is the prelude to a further birth. The frustration of desire is painful, as is separation from that which is desired, as is the sating of desire. . . . The origin of this universal suffering is the craving to exist, the craving for the pleasures that the five interior and the five external senses experience, and even the craving for death. Do you think that desires would exist were it not for ignorance, mother of all our ills?"

The breeze was so gentle that one would have believed it stirred by the soft wings of genii; the air was so pure that the dust seemed to have been filtered out by the foliage. The birds had hushed their songs so as not to cover the voice of the Blessed One.

"Now that the Four Noble Truths have been revealed to you, you must learn even more. What, O monks, is this Middle Path that the Tathagata has discovered, which unseals the eyes of the spirit, which leads to calm, to knowledge, to enlightenment, to Nirvana?

"Know that it lies precisely between the way of the world and asceticism; to abandon oneself to pleasure is ignoble and fruitless, mortification is painful and fruitless. . . . Know then that the path leading to peace is an Eightfold Path, and its branches are right understanding, right purpose, right speech, right action, right livelihood, right effort, right mindfulness, right concentration.

"This, O monks, is the sacred Truth concerning the cessation of pain.

"This, O monks, is the sacred Truth concerning the path that leads to the cessation of pain, the serene and free path.

"This, O monks, is the sacred Truth concerning the eight right activities that are unaffected by desire for the desirable or by fear of the fearful."

Sometimes one or another of the monks took advantage of a silence to speak up. Generally, it was not to formulate an objection but to put a question.

"How, O Blessed One, can the knowledge of truth free you from fear?"

"It sometimes happens that as you come from the river where you have been bathing, you step on a rope lying forgotten on the bank. You imagine you have brushed against a serpent, and your fear is so great that you immediately feel the poison stiffening your foot, your leg, your thigh. How great is your joy when you see that the serpent is only a wet rope! . . . Well, your terror, your agony, your impression of having been bitten—these are the effects of your error. Serenity comes to him who recognizes the illusion of his senses and who corrects his idea of what he believes to be his own personality; the causes of his suffering and his anguish are only the passing shadows of a dream."

"Then there is no such thing as personality?"

"There is no such thing. What you believe to be your 'I,' O Vashpa, is a moving river. What you are at this moment does not resemble what you were yesterday evening, and differs from what you will be tomorrow. A continuity of widely differing states—this is the law of impermanence, which you must understand. Turn your eyes from the 'You' and you will be delivered from evil."

This lesson, later called "The Sermon of Benares," lasted for many hours. The Scriptures, which were written down long afterward, tell us that time passed and no one noticed if it were day or night. Now and then a passer-by, attracted by a diffused glow, entered the park, sat down to listen to the golden voice, and lost any wish to continue his journey.

Kondinya, the eldest disciple, was the first to receive sanctification from the Buddha. For this reason, he was known, thereafter, as Anata, "He who has understood." Then came Ashvajit, Vashpa, Mahanaman, and, lastly, Bhadrika—he not being too quick-witted. These five masters, who came to be known as the Fathers, formed the first cell, which by now has expanded several hundred million times.

Word spread through Benares that a wise man was challenging and upsetting ideas then widely accepted. The Brahmans shrugged, for he was not of their caste; the Kshatriyas, on the other hand, were tempted to come to the Deer Park to hear him. A legend, popular among them, said that as long as the nobles kept the conduct of the kingdom in their hands, a saviour, if ever one appeared, would be born into the Kshatriya world.

Even those who, alerted by rumors rife in the city, came in a spirit of opposition and hostility were subdued. Thus, a young nobleman by the name of Yashas, who was as tormented as Siddhartha had been before him, came to sit behind the five masters. He never returned home, although a young wife awaited him there. Named Arhat the first day, because he absorbed the holy message so readily, he was the first layman to be admitted to the community.

Presently the disciples numbered sixty. Every afternoon, after they had taken their one frugal meal of the day, and every evening and on into the night, the Buddha expounded the Law. In order to rest his listeners, as much as to illustrate ideas that were sometimes very difficult to comprehend, he interspersed his teaching with anecdotes about his previous lives. One day, he addressed a man in the audience whom he recognized as a person involved in his earlier existences.

"Do you remember, Vinara, that hermit who ate so very little and yet was dying of hunger because a drought was ravaging the countryside? One day, he broke off his meditation to go down to look for food in the village, since the villagers no longer climbed up to his cave to bring him a bowl of boiled rice. . . . And do you remember how a hare jumped into his fire to be roasted—in this way, offering the ascetic some nourishment until the monsoon would turn the fields green again? . . . Well, that ascetic was you, Vinara, and I was the hare."

Vinara, who remembered no part of this, sat in openmouthed astonishment, and the Buddha added, with a smile, glancing at each of his listeners in turn, "I myself have lived five hundred and fifty times during this last cycle. But so have you. . . . You have been human beings, and according to whether you committed good or evil actions, had a pure or corrupt heart, conceived noble or vile thoughts, you were reborn nearer the gods whom you worship or, in the contrary case, much farther from them than men are. Reborn as pigs, for example, or even demons . . . For everything is paid for, every debt is settled. This is the law of Karma."

And, bowing their heads, the disciples meditated on the

implacable sentence: "No error can be redeemed. Man himself carves out the road that can, in the end, lead him where he need not be reborn."

Presently the Buddha decided to resume his journey northward. Before leaving, he called the monks together to give them his instructions. They would be spreading the Law, and the Master did not want them to expound its too arduous or forbidding points.

"This, O monks, is what you should teach the faithful.

"The Buddha has come to nourish the ignorant with wisdom, His doctrine is one of mercy purely; that is why it will be difficult for the powerful to learn. . . . As the sea is permeated with only one savor, that of salt, so the Law has only that of deliverance.

"Charity, knowledge, virtue, these are the possessions that cannot be squandered. To do a little good is worth more than to perform brilliant exploits. . . . A man is nothing if he does not do good to other creatures, if he does not console those who are lost. Do not forget that more tears have been shed than there are drops of water in this great ocean.

"Let the passions be subdued, as a straw hut is trampled by an elephant. Know also that he who would seek to flee from his passions in the sanctuary of a hermitage would live in error; he must fight them under the open sky, armed with healthy realities."

He emphasized, also, the profit of almsgiving.

"It is not profitable for you, monks. But, far more than a sacrificial offering of butter and honey, it is useful to him who gives to you. And you need not thank him for his alms; it is he who will be grateful to you for accepting them. If one wished to know how juicy is the fruit of charity, one would not eat a mouthful of food before one has given some away.

"Charity means, also, having compassion for animals. Prevent their being offered in sacrifice and ask that they be let go; let them find pasturage, water, and fresh breezes. . . ."

His last bits of advice were of a practical nature.

"Except to preach you will not mingle with the faithful, and you will have nothing to do with women. Be modest and chaste, avoid music, dancing, and perfumes. Accept nothing directly from another's hand into your own and refuse the smallest gift of money. Neither sell nor buy nor exchange anything whatsoever. . . . Take only one meal a day, in the morning, and be careful never to drink to excess.

"You will, perhaps, be insulted. Say to yourselves that your adversary is not your enemy; he is good, for he could have struck you. And if he strikes you, be grateful that he has not killed you. And if he makes an attempt on your life, know that you are dying for the faith and that it will be counted in your favor for your deliverance.

"And now, go out into the world, O monks!"

The Blessed One set out again on the road to Uruvilva, hoping to join some holy Brahmans in that city whose knowledge he had heard highly spoken of. Along the way he met some musicians looking for a woman who had made off with their few poor possessions.

"Would it not be more worth your while to seek yourselves?"

The three ballad singers guffawed at this, whereupon the Buddha asked one of the men to lend him his lute. When he plucked the strings, all of Nature seemed to find voice, as the instrument sounded the quavering calls of the blackbirds, the splashing of hidden springs, the trembling of leaves under the touch of the wind. Discovering that such sounds could be made to come from bronze threads strung across a wooden box, the musicians begged the Perfect One to teach them an art in which they had supposed themselves skilled.

"You thought you knew music, O brothers, and yet you

had only a coarse knowledge of it. In the same way, what do you know of yourselves? Yet you laughed when I advised you to seek yourselves!"

A long and penetrating monologue so completely persuaded the musicians that, henceforth, when the Buddha preached his Law, his words were always accompanied by a lute, a cithara, and a flute.

At last, the Blessed One had the opportunity to speak with the Kashyapa brothers. They were, indeed, three eminent Brahmans who, if possessed of immense erudition, were also possessed by boundless pride, which was constantly fed by the awed attentiveness of the thousand disciples whom they instructed. Imbued by a sense of their own holiness, they wore it rather like a halo about their persons. They received the Buddha not as an Enlightened One but as a learned doctor with whom they would enjoy conversing. After a few days, however, they did not conceal from their visitor that an evil serpent was disturbing their meditations and was even intruding upon their daily sacrifices. They did not actually see the monster, of course, but they sensed his presence so sharply that they sometimes felt his venom enter their very hearts.

With a few words, the Tathagata caused the unwelcome guest to withdraw, but contrary to all expectations, this only strained his relationship with the three masters. Unquestionably, his miracle made a great impression on the disciples and threatened to undermine their regard for the three professionals who had profited from it so long. In actuality, however, the point of difference reached down to far more profound roots; it was the function of the Brahman that placed the Illumined One in opposition to the brothers Kashyapa.

When the officiating priest covered his head with his scarf and arranged all the cups of soma on the altar in order to reconstitute a "second man" participating in the life of the gods, and thus was led back to the matrix of the Cosmos; when in the fire of Agni he reassembled all ten thousand eight hundred pieces of fragmented Purusha; and lastly, when he made himself divine, transmuting his senses to make them "perceivers" of knowledge, he could feel at his back the lucid appraisal of the Buddha. This guest was unquestionably a deeply learned man, but he felt no need to achieve godhood through the ritual of sacrifice, and this attitude was, quite simply, intolerable to the three masters.

They therefore undertook to discredit him in the eyes of the ashrama by demanding that he publicly perform other miracles. They selected as arbiter King Prasenajit, whose scrupulous objectivity was beyond dispute. "Perhaps this stranger does possess a certain wisdom," the brothers went about saying. "But he is too young for us to bow before him. First, let him prove that he possesses the eight supreme Siddhi."

The trial was conclusive. In the palace that the King of Kosala had ordered built for this confrontation, the Buddha rose in the air and shook the dust from his feet over the curled plaits of the Brahmans. With his glance alone, he caused the walls of the palace to burst into flames that consumed nothing; he then extinguished them with a shower of perfumed water. Shafts of multicolored lights transformed the air into one vast rainbow and, simultaneously, a profusion of blue lotus floated down from the sky, each bearing a miniature Buddha in its heart. Beginning with the King, everyone present fell to his knees. "Behold Indra, who has come to dwell among men." The three brothers, ashen-faced and humiliated, merely lowered their eyes and murmured a prayer.

The Buddha wanted no such easy victory. He was able to divine the inner thoughts of the eldest Kashyapa, and he realized that the man believed himself to possess the loftiest sanctity that a human being can achieve. The Buddha wanted to touch the heart of this rebel, who was so misled by pride. Taking him by the arm, he led him apart. "You think your holiness cannot be matched, O brother Kashyapa. And I say this to you, you are not on the path that leads to holiness, and you do not know how to follow the path that would lead you there. You must listen to me in order to dissipate the shadows in which you live."

The Brahman was annoyed that a thought he believed secret had been so easily detected. He reflected for a moment, but suddenly a feeling came over him that his snowy white loincloth, his sacred cord, and his combs had fallen to the ground at his feet, together with his presumption. Leading the Blessed One back among the astonished disciples, he fell to his knees before him.

"Teach me, O my Master. Guide me through the night where I walk."

And thereupon followed the Fire Sermon.

"Do you not perceive, O monks, that all things in the world are on fire? The eye is on fire, the ear is on fire, and all our senses are on fire."

Gentle and compassionate by nature, the Buddha seemed that day to speak like thunder.

"The fire of life must be put out. For everything in the world is enflamed by the fire of desire, the fire of hatred, the fire of ignorance. Birth, old age, death, cares, complaints, grief, sorrow, carnal love, all are on fire. . . . The things visible to thine eye, O Brahman, are on fire. The things audible to thine ear are on fire. And it is thus for each of thy five senses and thy interior senses.

"Then do you not conceive an aversion for your senses and for the things, the impressions, and the feelings that they arouse? If you do conceive an aversion, know then that you are delivered, that you are free of your passions. And understand, O Brahman, that birth is ended for you, and that this true holiness of which you used to speak will be achieved. All the rest is only illusion that devoured you like fire."

The Buddha realized that if he and his disciples were to travel far and wide to spread the Law, they would need a center where, during the rainy seasons when they could not get about, both disciples and novices could be instructed.

A rich banker established in Sravasti, by the name of Sudatra, had already presented the Buddha with some land, lying about twenty leagues distant from the capital city of Kosala. The man had bought the property from one Prince Jeta. The Prince, who lacked both heart and spiritual sensitivity, had demanded in payment as many pieces of gold as, placed side by side, would cover the whole expanse of the site. It was an outrageous price and the gold had had to be delivered by the cartfuls. But the merchant had been touched by the spirit of grace and raised no objection; resolved to consecrate his fortune to him who was bringing deliverance, he had not only purchased the land but also built dormitories, assembly rooms, refectories, and even a pavilion where the Saint might meditate in peace. No expense was too great if humanity might be delivered of its suffering. Lavish banquets were prepared so that even the faithful coming from great distances could be present and cared for. It is estimated that the merchant raised nearly a million gold lacs for his project.

Although the Buddha had smilingly composed a little verse

A man of sense
Who pays mind to his true interests
Should build beautiful retreats
And have wise monks live there

he did not seem completely happy about the comforts offered his disciples.

Nonetheless, the desire to emulate Sudatra's example spread like a contagion among the Sudras. The daughter of a Sravasti trader, for example, offered rain robes to the whole order so that the monks would not have to undress during the rainstorms to keep their clothing dry. She pledged, furthermore, that during her lifetime she would furnish meals for incoming and departing monks, special diets for the sick, and also would have meals brought to the nurses so that they would not have to leave their patients to beg for their own food. In addition to all these things, she offered medicines, rice pudding for all celebrations, and even suitable coverings for the use of decent women bathing in the river, so that they would not have to endure the quips of their fallen sisters.

The less wealthy Kshatriyas could not compete with the merchants. Nevertheless, they flocked in large numbers around the Buddha, perhaps because he belonged to their caste, perhaps because the Doctrine seemed to threaten the authority of the Brahmans. Tradition required a nobleman to end his earthly days by withdrawing from the world. But some Shakyas were so stirred by the teaching offered at the monastery of Jetadava that they did not await a ripe age to put on the yellow robe.

Devadatta and his brother Ananda, accompanied by some fellow warriors, also came to hear their cousin Siddhartha preach. They were curious and, at the same time, rather mistrustful, yet despite their reservations on arriving, they were also convinced by his words. In a single retreat, Bhadrika achieved knowledge of the Three Truths—the impermanence, pain, and vanity of all things. Anurud-Sha acquired the faculties of clairvoyance and clairaudience. Ananda attained the first of the four degrees of holiness. But Devadatta remained hostile. He derived no spiritual benefit from the instruction, but he rapidly absorbed more extensive knowledge than any layman had ever possessed. However, at one point when the Perfect One was questioning him, an ass began to bray. A god, perhaps, was poking fun at him?

The Perfect One kept his promise to King Bimbisara to return to Rajagriha; he went to live in the Perch Wood, not far from the capital. Two new disciples had joined the monks —Sariputra and Maudgalyayana. The former was a Brahman, and his conversion is a memorable one. He had encountered an elderly, yellow-robed monk and was struck by his remarkable serenity. When Sariputra inquired what master's teaching the monk had followed, he received the following reply:

Phenomena are born of a cause.
The Tathagata teaches what this cause is
And how to put an end to it.
That is what I learned from
The great Sramana.

This aroused the Brahman's curiosity, and he did not rest until he had heard the Buddha speak. Installing himself in the vihara in the Bamboo Grove, he became an ideal foil for the Master; he always asked precisely those questions that elicited the most profound replies. It is not surprising that, after the Buddha's death, it was this Sariputra and his inseparable friend who were inspired by the true spirit of the Doctrine to convoke the first Great Buddhist Council, which codified the Master's teaching.

Bimbisara came in person to greet his visitor. As the King stood bareheaded before the Monk and ignored Kashyapa, the voice of a Brahman rose sharply: "What a remarkable error for our great King to make. He mistakes the pupil for the master! See how he bows before Gautama and does not even glance at the revered Kashyapa."

But the King had already fallen to his knees, and he bowed until his forehead touched the ground between the Blessed One's feet. "O my master, teach them that I am thy disciple and thy servant. Speak and I will listen to thee, command and I will obey."

While the Buddha was explaining his mission, the King remained standing. At the end, he sat down on a seat lower than that of the Blessed One, and it was quite clear that he was happy in that humble position. But when he spoke his voice was roughened by emotion.

"In my youth, I hoped for five things. I hoped that I would become king; that my kingdom would some day receive a visit from an Enlightened One; that I would be able to sit in contemplation of this Illumined One; that he would teach me his Law; and that I would be able to confess my faith in him. Today I declare before all of you that I surrender to this man." He turned to the Buddha. "My refuge is in thee, Lord; my refuge is in thy Law; my refuge is in the Sangha, the community of thy monks."

A chorus of voices arose, chanting, "The gentle Master is with the meek. He brings deliverance and, like shining gold, he enriches Rajagriha." Bimbisara ordered a golden jug to be fetched, from which he poured water over the upturned palms of the Blessed One.

"I must see thee and hear thy holy message every day. . . . This place is too far from the capital. Allow me, Lord, to present thee with another. It is large, and thy disciples can live comfortably there. It is not too far from the city, so that thy monks can easily offer my subjects the joy of giving them alms. But it is not too near, so that they can meditate in the midst of Nature. As thy hands receive this water from my hands, so let the Bamboo Grove pass into thy possession."

The earth trembled. Henceforth, thanks to an impulse of the heart and not to money, the Law had soil in which to take root.

Book Six

I

FOR FORTY YEARS THE BUDDHA WAS TO GO FROM SOUTH TO north and again to the south, preaching, training disciples, founding religious communities, persuading kings and laborers, noblemen and merchants, to accept the Law.

The largest cities—Sravasti, Rajagriha, Gaya, Vaisali—the humblest market towns, and villages of only a few huts saw the Holy Monk arrive, seat himself on a stone, and talk gently to the people, drawing for them, in the dust of the road, the Wheel of Life and of Rebirth. Two centuries later, the great emperor Asoka commemorated these sermons by covering the countryside with stone columns on which he ordered engraved the principles of the Law. Believers and fol-

lowers of the Buddha built stupas to honor his miracles, to recall some episode from the Jataka, and to enshrine relics, thus
perpetuating the intricate network of the Buddha's travels in
this and his preceding lives.

In his own day, there was intense rivalry between the
capitals of the two states of Maghada and the Mallas. Rajagriha's reputation for wealth and even for luxury was known
far beyond the country's frontiers, and the city prospered under the rule of a spectacularly rich monarch. Vaisali flour-
ished thanks to its profitable trade, and was wisely administered by an oligarchic government under the monopolistic
control of the Licchavi family. At the beginning of every
year an uncle, a brother, and a cousin took over the reins of
government and by means of such a coalition, nipped in the
bud the ambitions of any candidates outside the clan.

Today, if one surveys the plain where a few wretched
villages vegetate around the present town of Besarh, it is hard
to imagine that here, in the fifth century B.C., the city of Vaisali numbered exactly seven thousand seven hundred buildings
surmounted by as many cupolas, that lakes and pools strung a
necklace of emeralds and sapphires around the city, and that
mango and banana groves encircled them like the setting for
precious jewels. A religious community had been established
in a park donated by the brilliant courtesan Amrapali. In the
center of the park, the monkeys had, with their own hands,
hollowed out a pool for the Buddha to bathe in. These quick-
footed, impudent thieves were so much under the influence of
their protector that they forgot to rob any orchards. The one
larceny they did commit was to steal the Blessed One's begging bowl, but it was only to bring it back to him, an hour
later, overflowing with wild honey.

The capital of Magadha prided itself on its fertile soil and
on its rice, which was of exceptional size and flavor, but it es-
pecially rejoiced in the possession of the most expensive cour-

tesan in all India. Sahavali demanded a hundred gold pieces—plus a fine jewel—for a single night. That was just twice the fee of her rival in Vaisali. It must be said that King Bimbisara himself had presided over the development of this beautiful woman's talents. By her he had a son, Jivaka, who went as a young man to the Punjab to study medicine. He became a most accomplished physician and returned home in time to cure the Perfect One of a stubborn intestinal weakness simply by making him inhale the fumes of a decoction of a hundred and eight herbs in which lotus leaves had been steeped. This incident gave the Master an opportunity to improve relations between the two capitals, which had been growing increasingly strained.

All was not smooth in the life of the Buddha. True, his followers were now counted in the thousands. His compassionate message had conquered hearts pure enough to understand it—almost without need of words. The miracles he performed as if he were playing a game overwhelmed the skeptical. At Sravasti, had he not caused the hands and feet of a nobleman to grow again, after King Prasenajit had unjustly tortured the man because he suspected him of having lured away a royal concubine? Did he not bring the dead back to life? Did he not extinguish fires by force of thought alone? One hostile Brahman, overcome at having misjudged such power, felt so deeply humiliated that he carefully tied a jug of sand around his neck and threw himself in a pond, where he drowned.

For the Buddha, however, as for his senior disciples, miracles were only one possibility implicit in the higher degrees of holiness. Maudgalyayana, for example, made an arduous journey to try in vain to persuade Sariputra to leave the place where he was living and return with him to the order, only to discover when he himself got back that his friend, traveling through the air, was quietly sitting at the feet of the Blessed One. Often the Master was obliged to oppose these spectacular demonstrations, for he considered it useless to abuse the extraordinary.

Although King Bimbisara continued to shower proofs of respectful friendship on the Tathagata, the nobles were becoming alarmed to see so many of their young sons desert their warrior calling to follow the teaching offered in the Bamboo Grove. Women clamored in protest through the streets, men stamped angrily on the roses that were strewn along the avenues to the palace whenever the Saint was coming to talk to the King. "Why has this son of the Shakyas come to us? Were there not enough monks already preaching virtue and the good life? How many of our wives must live like widows? How many fathers will have no son to close their eyes in death! A plague would take fewer children away from us!"

"Do not let these curses trouble you," the Buddha told his disciples again and again. "Simply answer: 'It is because the perfect ones know the Truth, the one Truth, that people listen to them and follow them.' The rest is simply the croaking of crazy frogs."

It was in Rajagriha that Devadatta and Crown Prince Ajatasatru (the latter, after his father's death, would lay waste to the kingdom of the Shakyas) made an elephant drunk and took off his chains just as the Buddha was entering the avenue to the royal palace. Terrified by the drums and trumpets, the myopic creature mistook flags and banners for enemies to be crushed, and losing all control, he rushed toward the happy group approaching him. There was panic. Guards vanished, spectators dived into the nearest doorways, flags were dropped from shaking hands and blanketed the ground, which trembled under the thundering gallop. Ananda threw himself before the Buddha, directly in the path of the

enraged beast. The Buddha raised three fingers. The elephant
paused uncertainly, shuddering, and peering left and right as if
to find its bearings. Then, its thick gray skin still rippling with
tension, it kneeled and throwing back its trunk, trumpeted
seven times. Ashen-faced, the Buddha's traitorous cousin and
the miserable Prince leaped on their horses and fled, cursing
under their breath.

Even the disciples occasionally created anxieties for their
Master, whether from excess of zeal or emotional instability.
Even the devoted Ananda—who had been born the night of
the Illumination—caused him a great many worries. The day
after Ananda's marriage, the bridegroom had found his cousin
at the door of his house; the Buddha was begging for his food,
and the young husband had hastened to fill his bowl with the
finest tidbits left from the wedding feast. But the Wise One
had smiled sadly, spilled the food on the ground, and walked
away without a backward glance.

The surprised young man had followed to the place
where the Buddha was preaching, and he was so deeply stirred
that he agreed to don the yellow robe and to have his head
shaved. Before long, however, he bethought him of his wife
and, one day when he was assigned to guard duty at the monastery, he decided to leave. He tried to close the gate carefully
behind him, but every time he pushed one of the portals shut,
the other immediately swung open as if it were being drawn
by a spring. This maneuver lasted the whole day. Night was
falling when the Buddha returned, conversing with his disciples. Ananda hid behind a tree, but just as the Master was passing by, the tree rose into the air and disclosed the abashed cul-
prit.

The Master was most forbearing; he did not ever repri-
mand his cousin, and Ananda did rejoin his young wife. He
spent the entire time with her extolling his Master and the dis-

ciples and the monastery, until the exasperated young woman scratched him or fell into a sulk and turned her back on him as they lay in bed. On the other hand, Ananda endlessly praised the young woman's charms to his Master. One day, when he was walking with Gautama, the young man felt urgently that he must go find her. But the Buddha read his true thoughts and made him see the charred remains of a she-monkey and then five hundred radiantly beautiful nymphs.

"What do you think of this scorched little beast?" he asked, without a trace or irony. "Is it as beautiful as the one you cherish?"

In no way amazed that the Master perceived his most fleeting and secret thoughts so readily, Ananda exclaimed, "She can no more be compared to those ravishing goddesses than can that horrible carcass."

And he walked away, deep in thought, quite won back to his monk's calling. Afterward, whenever he lost himself in meditation, his comrades teasingly asked him which nymph he had chosen.

Unremitting opposition to the Buddha came from the Jains. This ascetic sect developed in a parallel way to Buddhism; the Jains also claimed to win salvation by renunciation, non-violence, and holiness. To signify their detachment from the world, they gave up clothing and walked about completely naked. They were jealous of the Perfect One's fame and had one dream—to discredit him. A courtesan lent herself to one plot against him.

Every evening for a month, this woman, Sinca by name, put on a revealing scarlet sari trimmed with a broad band of gold thread, and went ostentatiously to the park of Jetavana, where the Buddha was accustomed to rest in an isolated cottage. When people asked ironically if she were going there to be converted, she replied, "What is it to you where I go?"

And in the mornings, as she returned, she would say in a voice at once weary and exultant, "It's no business of yours where I'm coming from." No one knew that she had spent the night alone in an abandoned hut, and the scandalous gossip was rife.

As the months passed, people were astonished to see her lose her slender figure and begin to walk heavily. One morning, she appeared in the midst of a sermon in which the Buddha was explaining the Law as some several hundred listeners followed him with bowed heads. She tugged boldly at the Buddha's scarf and, with a vulgar gesture, motioned to her rounded belly. "You know very well how to enjoy the pleasures of love," she cried piercingly, "but when are you going to trouble yourself about this child of yours who will soon be born?"

Indra felt his throne grow hot—the unfailing sign of danger. Accompanied by four archangels, he slipped down to earth. There, his four companions transformed themselves into mice, which scurried under the courtesan's sari. In a matter of seconds, they nibbled through the strings that were holding up a small block of wood wrapped in cloth; it fell on Sinca's toes.

"There is your child," said the Master, laughing, "born already!"

There was a tremendous scandal. People spat in the shameless woman's face, they hurled handfuls of dust and mud at her, and she fled followed by a volley of stones. Angry hands snatched at her garments, and by the time she had escaped from the monastery she was almost naked. Indra, who had taken the affair into his own hands, caused the earth to open under the miserable creature's feet the moment she was outside Jetavana. A huge flame shot up, enveloped her in a burning sheath, and sank down, dragging her with it into the fiery regions of hell.

II

KING SUDDHODANO HAD GREATLY AGED. HIS BEARD WAS GRAY, his back was bent, and his limbs felt wearier when he awoke than when he lay down to rest. It was not so much the years that had aged him as disappointment. He saw his own days coming to an end, and he despaired of Siddharta's returning to occupy the throne. He had, of course, heard of the holiness his son had attained, but precisely because he knew that the Prince now possessed prodigious wisdom, knowledge, and power, the King clung to the hope that this accomplished man would devote himself, at last, to the well-being of the kingdom of the Shakyas.

Accordingly, he sent a messenger to him, in Rajagriha.

When the man arrived at the Bamboo Grove the Buddha was preaching. "An evil man laid a snare in a forest toward which he drove a herd of deer by cries and shouts, calculating that the beasts would wallow helplessly in the miry ground and die of starvation. But another man happened by, who cleared a path from the swamp to the firm and safe pasturage of a nearby mountain.

"Do you not understand, O brothers, that as the animals were deceived by the snare, so men deceived by Mara risk drowning in pleasure and perishing in ignorance? He who opens to them the way to salvation is the blessed Enlightened One; that man is I. It is up to you, now, to climb to the clear summit of the mountain."

The messenger felt his heart swell with joy. Quite forgetting his mission, he threw himself at the Buddha's feet. "Accept me among thy disciples, O Master!"

As he heard the reply "Come then, monk," he felt his hand clutch a begging bowl. And just as his clothes miraculously assumed the shape and color of monastic garb, so his features suddenly became those of an elderly religious.

When Suddhodano received no news of his messenger, he supposed that the man had perished before ever reaching Siddharta, and he sent a second. Eight times he dispatched a man to fetch back his son, and eight times it happened that the messenger found himself won over to the Saint and clothed in the yellow robe. In the same way, the bees, when they discover the flowers of the mogras, become drunk and forget their responsibility to gather honey for the hive. Finally, the King appealed to Uyadin, one of the Prince's comrades in his youth.

"In the old days you were his best friend, and I know no one whom he should receive more warmly than you. Tell him how sad I am, make him understand what I long for so greatly. The gods grant that he may be touched by what you say! I will give you a thousand of my finest troops as a body-guard on your journey."

But as Uyadin traveled toward Rajagriha, he heard so fervent a eulogy of his old playfellow that he had no need to talk with the monks he met or to reach Rajagriha to know that he, also, would be counted among the Master's disciples. Even before approaching the Blessed One, with eager heart and mind he cast off his clothes, donned the saffron robe, and had his hair and eyebrows shaved; his entire escort promptly followed suit.

Later, however, when Uyadin was alone and on the verge of sleep, the words of his lord returned to his mind; he was moved, and he said to himself, "Tomorrow I will remember to speak to the Master and tell him about his father's grief. Pity will surely persuade him to visit Kapilavastu."

Tomorrow, tomorrow . . . alas, it was always tomorrow. The impulse to speak was forgotten until one day, at the end of a sermon, Uyadin noticed a resemblance between an elderly Brahman and his sovereign, which served to remind him, while in the Master's presence, of his mission.

"The sap runs in the trees, O Blessed One, and the leaves are about to unfurl anew. See how the gentle sun of spring shines through the budding branches. The season is good for traveling; it is no longer cold, it is not yet hot. The earth has turned a smiling green, and along the way we will find food. . . . Yes, Master, the season is good for traveling."

"Why are you urging me to travel, Uyadin?" the Buddha asked, with infinite sweetness. But before his disciple could reply, the Perfect One laid his hand on the head that leaned trustingly against his knee. "I will go to Kapilavastu and I will see my father. It is my duty—as it is my wish."

King Bimbisara was depressed to have the Buddha leave his kingdom. He had a painful presentiment that the Master would never return to expound some point or other of the Law to him; he did not feel that his own conversion was complete, and he proposed setting out with his Master as a humble monk. The Blessed One had almost to force him to remain on his throne, both to prevent the kingdom's slipping into the impatient hands of Prince Ajatasatru and to protect and spread the Faith.

The Buddha himself turned back with a feeling of sadness, as he reached the top of one of the almost perpendicular hills that dominated the city. His glance wandered over the roofs, the monumental gates, the broad, straight avenues, the eight square towers of the citadel, and the winding network of narrow streets. Pensively, he contemplated the patch of green that was the Bamboo Grove. Turning with visible emotion to Ananda, he made no attempt to conceal that he still felt attached to earthly things or that he saw the end of his last earthly life approaching. "This is the last time I will see the diamond throne and the royal villa," he said quietly but with a sigh.

Five men had heard that first sermon in Benares. Sixty monks had left the Deer Park, and a thousand had crowded around the Master in Jetavana, in Vaisali. Now, ten thousand monks from Kosala and Maghadha, all with shaven heads and wearing the saffron robe, followed the Buddha along the road leading up to Kapilavastu. A company of such size can travel only very slowly, for frugal as the monks' regime was, some nourishment had still to be provided. For this reason, they advanced only one league a day.

Uyadin, whose degree of holiness enabled him to move rapidly through the air, did not lose an hour before flying off to Kapilavastu; he must inform the King that his son had set out on his journey.

"Ah, here you are at last, my dear Uyadin. I was afraid

that you had not been able to carry out your mission, or that the robe you have put on had made you forget it. . . . Now I can dry my tears."

And when the messenger refused the succulent feast that was to celebrate the good news, the King cried, "I want you to owe your daily food to me. I want my son to owe his to me, also, for the duration of the journey he has undertaken to please me. So, eat here and you will take a part of our meal to Siddhartha."

Uyadin seized the flagon a servant was offering him and threw it into the air, watching as it sailed off in the direction of the south. A few moments later, the precious object came to earth at the feet of the Blessed One. For two months—the slow journey lasted that long—Uyadin went daily to the royal palace to find food for the Master.

It is claimed that the Buddha completed the last two leagues of the trip by flying through the air, and that he was accompanied by heavenly musicians who melted away like fog when he alighted on the earth. However that may be, from the moment the Perfect One crossed the Ganges, excitement in Kapilavastu mounted to fever pitch. Many citizens were unable to contain their impatience and set out on foot on a two-week march to discover for themselves just how their Prince looked. They listened to him preach and, afterward, those who still felt enough attachment to worldly things to resist the joy of wearing the saffron robe, came back to the city full of talk about this man who seemed to move surrounded by a halo of light. Despite their enthusiasm, they did not succeed in convincing the nobles. The Shakyas stiffened with pride.

"Are not many among us older than Siddhartha? And why should we pay homage to him? For a hundred generations, our families have built the glory of the kingdom, stone by stone. Let the children, let the young people bow before him; his elders will meet him with heads high."

Accordingly, they took no part in the preparations for the celebration. But the rest of the city was topsy-turvy with excitement, from the palace to the outlying districts where the peoples of low caste were relegated. Five hundred elephants had their heads decorated with scrolls painted red and blue, and their tusks sheathed in gold. Banners were planted along the streets, fragrant branches were scattered over the roadways, and houses were decorated with leafy boughs and wreaths of flowers. The bayaderes were instructed to rehearse the dances they would perform at the head of the procession. Baskets were heaped with roses and jasmine, to be strewn over the Prince's route at the last moment so lavishly that his charger Kantala would sink knee-deep in their fragrance. Silken pavilions were raised at every crossroad so that the traveler might rest his wearied limbs before entering the city.

The third sabbath of the month having arrived, people arose before dawn. They wanted to be ready, the moment they heard the elephants trumpeting, the drums beating, and the bells sounding, to scramble up trees and have a clear view of the approaching caravan. But as far as eye could see, the road lay empty. The sun climbed high in the sky, flowers wilted, and disappointment covered the people's joy like ashes.

Then a poor monk, dressed in a much patched robe and followed by two disciples, appeared in the quarter of the Untouchables. He went from door to door, wordlessly holding out his bowl, which was shaped like a gourd. He was so majestic of mien, his manner commanded such respect and exuded such goodness that people knelt at his feet, offered what they had, and then hurried to their houses to find some further morsel, chagrined that they were so poor. A group formed gradually and followed in the footsteps of this unknown rishi.

People whispered to each other, "Who is he? We never have seen an ascetic like this." The procession numbered several thousand people by the time it entered the royal city, and it included only the lowest, despised caste.

A very, very elderly Brahman who, years ago, had been present at one of the young Prince's lessons, recognized Siddhartha. Choosing a short cut, he ran as fast as his trembling old legs would carry him to warn the King that his son was arriving—not as a glorious prince but as a beggar fed by the defiled Untouchables. Raging disappointment drove all love from the King's heart. He spat three times on the ground and tore his silver beard in anger. Then, scowling darkly, he mounted his horse, magnificently caparisoned in scarlet and green, and flicking its sides with his spurs, he galloped through streets thronged by his astonished subjects. The guards had no time to shout "The King! The King! On your knees!" before the dust from the stallion's hooves was settling in his rider's wake.

But when Suddhodano saw his son look at him with meekness and filial respect, he completely forgot to upbraid him for not coming on horseback, surrounded by glittering lances and all the honors due a prince. Deeply moved, he took a few steps toward the poor, resplendent monk. "My son! . . . Art thou then my son?" he murmured, and he bowed his gray head. The nobles who had raced to catch up with him stared haughtily at the newcomer. But, to their surprise, they felt an invisible hand seize them by the shoulders and force them to their knees.

Walking on together, isolated in their joy, father and son proceeded toward the garlanded pavilion where the Prince was to receive the homage of his people. But the Blessed One protested. "It is not Siddhartha who has returned, O my father, but the preacher of Justice and of Truth. The ties that bound you to the son you have lost must henceforth unite you in love with all beings."

"But if this is what you intend, why did you not come back as a ruler?"

"Because, Father, it is the custom of my race."

"Your race can count a hundred thrones in its history since the time of Maha Sammat, but never an action such as yours. Never have there been beggars in our lineage," the King rejoined, with a gesture of anger.

Sitting down on the throne of gold that had been prepared for him, the Blessed One replied gravely, "I am not speaking of my mortal descent but of the invisible line from the Buddhas past to those to come. I am one of them, and what they have done in the past I do today; what takes place today has already happened before. . . . Once upon a time there was a king who came in splendid armor to welcome his returning son who was dressed as a hermit. With love and humility the son offered his father the finest of all the treasures he had brought back from his long and grueling travels."

To illustrate his own mission, the Buddha went on to relate at length the story of Prince Visvantara. This young man had been exiled by his father, King Sanjaya, for having offered the Rajah of Kalinga a marvelous elephant that had the power to make the rain fall. The loss of this miraculously endowed animal would be a disaster when the dry season came and turned the soil to dust.

Setting out in a chariot with his wife and two children, Visvantara responded to the requests of the Brahmans he met by handing over, successively, his chariot, his horse, the princess's jewels, their clothing, his son, his daughter, and, finally, his wife. Could a man refuse any possession whatever to one who expressed a need of it? At last, the prince, stripped of all that can attach a man to life, found himself in a forest, alone, naked, wizened, possessing only the faculty of thought.

Indra was watching over him, however, and when he realized that Visvantara had passed through the shadows that veil the human eye and spirit, he caused the royal children, wife, and the exiled prince to be found again by the king. Restored to the court, the hermit renounced his claim to the throne forever, preferring to instruct his father's subjects in the truths he had discovered.

"Now," continued the Blessed One, "I am Visvantara. You acclaim me as his people once acclaimed him. Just as he urged his father's subjects to follow the road that leads to Deliverance, today I invite you to follow the straight path. . . . I will lift veil after veil for you. . . . The stars wheel through the heavens, and life, joy and death endure. The flux and reflux of mutable existence flow like a river whose waves, whether swift or slow, follow one upon another, forever the same yet always different, from their remote source to the far-distant ocean where they find rest. . . . Listen to my words, and your hearts will know peace."

When the Buddha had finished speaking, a prodigious silence prevailed, although tens of thousands of people were gathered together in the royal park. Subdued—and certain among them profoundly touched—the Shakyas bowed low to the Holy One before they withdrew, deep in reflection.

No one, however, had thought to offer the Saint his meal for the morrow.

III

THE NEXT DAY, AS THE BUDDHA WALKED THROUGH THE STREETS, crossing one threshold after another to beg his food, Gopa Yasodhara, sitting behind a curtained window, saw her husband pass by. She turned pale; her heart was in a tumult, and she could not keep from singing softly to herself:

Shining and dark are the ringlets of his hair.
Spotless and pure as the sun is the mark of his brow.
Straight and long is the delicately tapering nose
Of the heroic lion haloed in rays of gold.

Gopa was still beautiful. Her expression was now grave, her slender body was that of a mature woman, but her movements had lost none of their grace, her eyes still glowed, and her mouth was bewitchingly alluring. This morning, in order to be more like the man she loved, she had discarded her bracelets and necklaces, unbound her hair, and putting aside her delicate gowns, had donned a coarse, reddish robe; she had not tinted her palms or nails with henna, yet she looked more seductive than when elegantly groomed.

She stood, now, motionless behind the screen, oblivious of the servant who was urging her to go down into the courtyard where the great door had been deliberately left open. Only when Maha Prajapati came looking for her did she rouse herself.

"No," she said firmly. "No, I will not go with you. I do not know if I deserve to see my husband. But if I have led a virtuous life and done no wrong, he will come to me himself. Then I will show him all the respect that is his due. . . . I will wait for him!" she whispered, with an inaudible sob.

She gave orders that her bed of down be removed and replaced by three wooden planks. The garlands of fresh flowers were taken down, the jars of perfumes and powders were emptied into a brook; a tallow torch replaced the balsam oil lamps. The cook was instructed to prepare only one meal a day, of fruit and vegetables.

Then, one day, the Buddha came. Alone and unannounced, he entered the room where she sat knitting a scarf of saffron wool. Without a word he sat down; without a word she rose, knelt before him, threw her beautiful arms around his ankles, and laid her forehead on his dusty feet. The Wise One bent his head over her with tender respect.

"The greatest man is as open to love as the most humble. . . . Three eras of heavy trials have made me understand that giving myself completely to you, as I did, and giving myself to all men, as I do today, is like a laughing lake compared to a vast ocean. And so, my sister, my love for you has only be-

come greater for having been freed from the snares of the senses; it enfolds you in the cloak that shields all living beings. You have been my wife so often in past existences, and I will not forget that your tenderness has always marked out my path for me—even when I have had to leave you."

A new light glowed in Gopa Yasodhara's eyes and dried her tears. And, that night, she took her first steps on the road to eternal peace.

Someone in the palace—who no one knows—advised Rahula to go to his father and demand a share of the "treasure" all Kapilavastu was talking about. It was probably some stupid nurse who had misunderstood Gopa when she used to say to her son, "Your eyes shine just like Siddhartha's when I first knew him. Will you grow up to be as splendid as he was? He was as handsome as the gods of heaven. Love your father, Rahula, love him, and be worthy of the holy inheritance he will bequeath you. Once upon a time, your father possessed immense wealth—gold and jewels and more tunics than there are days in the year. You see him today going from house to house to beg his food, but don't think that he is poor. He has found a wonderful treasure."

Treasure! To the vulgar mind, this meant only one thing, and the women who bathed the child must often have gossiped about it. In any event, Rahula did go, in all innocence and confidence, to find the Perfect One. He went up to him and said, "Monk, it is good to stand in your shadow." The Wise One looked at him with such tender affection that he grew bolder.

"I am your son, my lord. I know that you possess the richest of all treasures. You must give me my share of the inheritance."

The Master did not answer. With a smile, he continued on his way, holding out his beggar's bowl, which the women, careful not to brush against him, filled with rice and herbs. Hardily the boy persisted, "I am more than seven years old and I have a right to it. They've told me so. I want my share of the inheritance!"

Having sat down to eat, the Buddha finally answered. "Are you sure what kind of treasure it is? Gold, jewels, rare weapons, rich garments, perhaps? How perishable are the things that vanity worships and that the bitter hunger for death causes the falsely rich to delight in! . . . You do well to claim your part of the inheritance, and I will indeed give you my seven jewels. . . . You will see the true worth of faith and purity, modesty and humility, obedience, renunciation and, most glorious of all, wisdom. Come, I will put you in the care of the holy Sariputra, who will make these treasures sparkle before your eyes."

King Suddhodano was deeply disappointed to see his grandson diverted from the throne and promised to the monastery, and he hid his chagrin by losing his temper. As a consequence, the Perfect One agreed that, in the future, children would be admitted to the novitiate only with the permission of their parents.

"Bear your grief in silence. Be like the elephant that is wounded in battle by the javelin but keeps its footing and will not groan. . . . We live in perfect joy who in the midst of ailing men are without ailment, who in the midst of harassed mankind know no weariness, who possess nothing. . . . The monk preserves a spirit that is filled with peace and enjoys a happiness that is denied miserable mankind."

For months Maha Prajapati went to wait for the Master at the door of the forest house near Kapilavastu where he was living. Dressed in rags and with great tears in her eyes, she stood there, hoping that the man whom she had brought up as a child would deign to look at her. Then, growing bolder, she dared put her request before him three times.

"How am I to live in a world whose joys I now know are false? My embroidered veils weigh upon me, my diadems, my bracelets, my necklaces wound me. Grant me the grace of joining the order. I know many other devout women who are ready to follow my example; for them the city is henceforth filled with shadows."

The Buddha was silent, as if he had not heard, so she went to find Ananda and begged him to intercede for her. He promised to try to help her but scarcely thought that he would succeed. He remembered clearly how the Buddha had answered him, in Vaisali, when he had suggested admitting women to the Buddhist order: "Unfathomable and dissembling, like the course of a fish through the waves—such is the nature of woman. She is as ferocious as a bandit, and as wily. Seldom does she tell the truth; to her truth is the same as untruth; she does not distinguish the false from the true. . . . Yes, one must be wary of women; for one as good and virtuous as Gopa there are a thousand and one who are frivolous, malicious, or vicious."

But now Ananda spoke so eloquently and with such heartfelt warmth that the Master, who had been hesitating for months, finally although reluctantly agreed.

"On ten conditions, Ananda. Every nun, even were she to have observed the rules of the order for a hundred years, shall rise in the presence of a monk, even were he a novice of a day's standing. She shall reside near a monastery of monks but she shall never enter it. She shall follow the instructions of the monks concerning her retreats, her twice monthly public confessions, and her attendance at sermons. Her breaches of conduct shall be absolved in a ratio of three to four, as compared to the monks. Before being admitted to the order, women shall be required to prove their virtue and steadfastness for a period of two years. They shall hold no discourse with the monks and shall refrain from addressing any spiritual exhortation to them."

Later, in the face of scandals that were corroding the Church, the Buddha was forced to express his disillusionment: "If women had not been admitted to the order, Ananda, chastity would have been preserved and the faith would have endured, strong and serene, for a thousand years!"

Nevertheless, women did offer the Tathagata frequent opportunities to manifest his power through rapid conversions or miracles. A slave girl from Sravasti was converted by the simple act of filling his begging bowl. A pretty woman by the name of Suprabha who had rejected her lovers in order to follow the Buddha's teaching was ravished by them; transformed into a swan, she flew up toward heaven. As the dancer Kuvalaya adroitly shed her garments, one by one, in the course of a whirling dance, she did not realize that she was losing more and more of her beauty with each discarded veil; at last, naked and wasted away, she repented with such genuine contrition that the Buddha agreed she might enter the order. Then there was the case of Virupa, the wife of the merchant Ganga; this wretched woman, although she was the daughter of King Prasenajit, was so ill-favored that her husband would allow no one to see her and, in despair, she hanged herself. Fortunately, a monk entered the house to beg and came upon this heartbreaking scene. He loosened the rope, comforted the woman, and went to inform his lord. By force of thought alone, the Perfect One mercifully bestowed surpassing beauty on the forsaken woman.

And, lastly, there is the charming story of the young girl who was too poor to contribute a mite to the collection that the rich merchant Anathapindaka had organized in Sravasti for the benefit of the Buddhist order. She could think of nothing to offer but the one dress on her back, the only thing she owned. When the collector passed down her street, ringing his little bell, she threw her robe down to him through a window, and then, mortified by her own nakedness, she hid. But Indra knew that the Buddha had been touched by her action; he caused the young girl to be dressed in sumptuous robes and bedecked with jewels worthy of a princess. Then, the following night, he led her directly into his paradise of the Thirty-three.

The Buddha—whom the entire city called Shakyamuni, or the Wise Man of the Shakyas—could linger no longer in Kapilavastu. There were so many, many people who must hear the word and who, perhaps, if only they knew how to listen, would be delivered thereby. Before leaving, he led all his people to the ruins of what had been, in ancient times, a great palace of the kingdom. He wanted to speak to them in the midst of those crumbled walls that could testify how even the greatest earthly splendor perishes.

That day Gopa Yasodhara dressed her hair with care; her choicest jewels emphasized the fine lines of her throat, wrists, and ankles. She wore her most beautiful sari, of blue and silver lamé, and seated at the feet of the Master, she spread its brilliant folds over the knees of her lord. She loved him more now, perhaps, than when he had been her husband.

With Rahula propped between his knees, the Buddha spoke for a long time, tracing the implacable Wheel of Life that no man can retard or halt. He spoke of the Uncreated Power, without features or feelings, that unfailingly regulates the progress of the world. He stated the Four Noble Truths through which he had attained Enlightenment, and he indicated the Noble Eightfold Path to salvation.

An impressive silence had settled over the people as they crowded closely around the speaker. It was not a heavy silence but an uplifted, a happy silence. . . . The women did not feel compelled to share every thought with each other and even forgot to capture and tuck into their chignons the rebellious locks of hair that were gently lifted by the evening breeze. The minds of the men were freed of daily preoccupations—concern for the harvest or shop, the pursuit of prestige—and all bitterness and greed had vanished. The children sat quietly, without a thought of play; nursing infants lay contentedly in their mothers' arms and not one of them even whimpered. Smiling, Rahula looked with mingled amazement and admiration at the imposing figure of his father and hung on every word he said.

May Amitabha be our witness! It is impossible to convey with a mere pen and in worldly speech what the Master said in that soft Indian twilight. The whole of Nature shared in the compassion and limitless love that filled every word. The snowy peaks of the Himalayas had turned a rosy gold, and the green-verdured slopes rippled in the gentle wind. Animals had come out from the thickets: the gray fox sat trustingly among men, the panther forgot the presence of the deer, the rhinoceros forbore to grunt, a wild elephant permitted a pair of tigers to crouch between its feet. Bats flew overhead, and no woman thought to cover her hair.

The light of day lingered well beyond the usual hour; night came, yet the air remained clear. Between the plain and the mountain darkness hung suspended like a sky maiden transfixed with love: the clouds were the massed tresses of her hair; the stars, the pearls and diamonds of her crown; the breeze, her choicest perfume.

"This Uncreated Power both kills and saves with no purpose other than to fulfill destiny. Death and suffering are the shuttles of its loom, love and life are its threads. It weaves and unweaves all things, corrects all things. Be just and it will reward you; be unjust and you will receive the wages of your wrongdoing—even if the Law is slow to make itself felt. For time does not count with the Law. Neither does it know anger or forgiveness. Its balance is unerring. This is the doctrine of karma."

Looking down over the multitude, the Blessed One offered guidance in human conduct.

"Be merciful and respect all life, no matter how lowly. Smother all malice, greed, and anger in your hearts.

"Give and receive freely, but take nothing wrongfully by means of violence, fraud, or falsehood.

"Never lie, even on occasions that seem to you to absolve the lie.

"Avoid drugs and strong drink that trouble the mind.

"Respect the wife of another and commit no carnal act that is illegitimate or unnatural.

"These are the five rules for your daily life."

The moon was at its zenith when, rising to his feet, he concluded:

"Avoid every offense in regard to the dharma, be mindful of the karma that establishes the destiny of man, and control your senses. This is Right Doctrine.

"Have right feelings, so that your existences may be like a gentle breeze that passes. This is Right Intention.

"Watch over your lips as if they were the portals of a palace wherein dwells a king; no unkind or impure word should soil them. This is Right Speech.

"Let every action combat a fault or foster a virtue. As one perceives the silver thread through the crystal beads of the necklace, so let love be seen through your good deeds. This is Right Conduct.

"There are loftier heights, of course, but these can be scaled only by feet that need no longer tread the highways of the earth. You must try to fly toward the sun only when your wings are strengthened by sturdy feathers. Live, therefore, as men have always lived, with wife and children, rejecting neither friendship nor pleasant diversions—but live so as to make of your weakness a golden ladder. By climbing one rung higher each day, you will finally leave the realm of false appearances behind, and you will discover new virtues that are even more worthy of being cherished and heights still more serene. . . . So live that you help the law of love to reign on earth. In this way you will one day attain freedom from rebirth, and you will be spared suffering forever."

He wound the folds of his scarf closely around his arm and, without another word, he walked away. Sitting on the ground, people did not raise their heads to see him go, for the words he had spoken kept his presence alive among them. Only the King stood up. Slipping off his sandals in token of humility, he kissed the border of the Wise One's robe as he passed. "Accept me, my son, as the most humble and the least of thy disciples."

For an entire month a golden glow lighted the spot where the Buddha had sat, and a stupa was erected later at the site. But, with time, the trunks of great trees began to push aside stones that had long been ruins; fewer and fewer men ventured into the heart of the dense forest to worship at the holy place, and its radiance is preserved only in memory.

Shakyamuni left his father's capital followed by a large group of proud Kshatriyas of his own blood. The nobles had discarded their weapons and splendid tunics, and dressed in the saffron robe, barefooted, with hair and eyebrows shaved, they humbly followed the Guide they had chosen, preferring a rigorous life of meditation to a gilded existence the desolating emptiness of which they could now assess.

By short stages, the Master led them southward, to one or another of the monasteries that kings and the governors of cities had liberally offered the monks. It often happened that the party would pause in a woods or by the border of a field, and would listen the whole night long to the Blessed One speak. Like a stone thrown into a lake, his words set up waves of concentric circles that widened to include all the disciples grouped around him. Neither fatigue nor sleepiness weighed on them, and fresh strength enlivened their minds and bodies when the time came to resume their journey. With a friendly gesture, the Buddha would brush aside the barrage of questions that exploded with all the energy pent up during the hours of instruction. In one such instance, he rose to his feet and tore a fistful of leaves from the tree under which he had been preaching.

"Where, do you think, are there more leaves? In my hand, or on the branches of all the trees in this forest? . . . I am holding very few between my fingers, am I not, compared to those that you see or that you do not see rustling in the breeze?

"Well, what I have discovered is infinitely more vast than what I reveal to you. If I have not taught you everything, it is because that would be of no profit to you. On the contrary, it would remove you from earthly things before you yourselves felt the need to be freed of them. I am here only to point out the way to salvation. It is for you to follow that way after meditating and divining for yourselves what I have deemed useless to teach you."

Nanda, the son of Maha Prajapati and the half brother of Siddhartha, had been named heir to the throne in place of Rahula. A bright future lay before him, and it beckoned to him all the more joyously since he was to marry Sundarika, a captivatingly beautiful girl with whom he was passionately in love. Yet he also followed the Master's call.

"How can you be full of joy when you are surrounded by shadows? Do you not see that death is always there, poised to descend on you no matter how you laugh and sing? As you have wandered from existence to existence, you have shed more tears than there is water in all the rivers and all the seas of this world. Ah! Nanda, let the world be worth no more to you than a fleck of foam! Let it be only a dream, and you will escape death!"

But if Nanda willingly turned away from the prospect of a throne and the heavy responsibilities of government, he was not long in regretting Sundarika. He was depressed by his own loss and by the grief he had caused her. At the same time, he was humiliated to see that the monks withheld their pure-hearted affection from him. Guided by the Master, he was gradually able to quench his desire. But Mara was always alert for the slightest faltering. "Well," he whispered, "haven't you become a true saint? Why do you let your brother outshine you?" Seduced now by pride, the young Prince cut himself a robe as long as the Blessed One's. It gave him childish pleasure to have people mistake him at a distance for Shakyamuni and rise respectfully to greet him. Before long, he took offense that his companions would sit down again when they recognized him. Informed of this, the Buddha rebuked him tartly. "What do you mean by such audacity? Do you believe that such behavior is likely to instill faith in those who do not yet have it, or to strengthen faith in those who do? You will shorten your robe at once, Nanda." Turning to the others, he added, "Any monk who sews himself a robe to my measure will be committing a grave misdemeanor and will be censured for it by the order,"

The Enlightened One had also to cope with numerous difficulties arising from the monks' lack of discipline. Discord broke out when he was preaching at Kombasi. In the course of a monk's public confession, the man refused to admit that he was guilty of a venial sin for which others reproached him.

Some monks supported him in his stubbornness; others condemned him severely for exploiting a subtle dialectic to exculpate himself. The injunction "Be obedient to the Law" he skillfully countered with "Tolerance is a virtue that the Master recommends we practice."

In an effort to calm them, the Blessed One urged the disputants to forget their respective grievances and join together for the sake of their holy mission. Some incomprehensible aberration caused several disciples to retort, "Keep quiet, Master, and stop pestering us with your preaching. You have managed to learn the Law. Very well, meditate on it. We are sure that your meditations are charming indeed. But we know perfectly well how to find our own way. Meditate, Master, and stay out of our quarrels. Out of respect for you, you understand, we do not want you to mix in them."

The Blessed One did not insist. He recalled having seen recently in the forest an old elephant use his powerful feet to scoop out a trench so that the water from a swamp could reach the herd. Far from being grateful to him, his kin shouldered him roughly aside and with their trunks they beat his ears—the ears of an elephant, as everyone knows, are very sensitive; finally, they drove him out of the herd. Accordingly, with a heavy sigh the Master took his begging bowl and set out for a humble village where he loved to go into retreat with his favorite disciples. He was not too surprised, a few months later, to see a delegation of monks from the opposition arrive, led by the man who had been responsible for the quarrel. The monks looked woefully thin and their eyes were as dull as those of a dead carp. The villagers, knowing that the Master had abandoned them, had refused to give them food. But the mistake that is confessed must always be forgiven and forgotten. . . .

It was perhaps during this estrangement that the Buddha created a double of himself. He decided to leave this double on earth so that men would not be alarmed by his absence, while he himself ascended to the abode of the gods. "My mother is calling me and I must teach her my Law, for she will have to be reborn. I will stay with her for three months. However, I will come down to earth once every day, and Sariputra—he alone—will know where to find me. I will give him my orders, and he will direct your conduct."

Everything furnished the Buddha with an opportunity to relate his teaching to the little events of daily life. If he saw a woman carrying a heavy basket on her head, he pointed her out to the disciples.

"At the beginning of life, our basket is empty and, little by little, we fill it with our desires without realizing that its weight is increasing, and its burden makes our path hard to travel. Let us therefore empty our basket, and our journey will be light, for without desire there is no suffering. Love will sustain our hearts, and one life will suffice for us to travel the road that leads to deliverance."

If a puff of wind blew out a lamp, the Perfect One would explain: "The flame should have lasted until there was no more oil. Then one could have refilled the bowl and re-lighted the wick. But the wind got there first. Ananda, relight the lamp and tell me how many flames there have been. Two, is it not so? In one sense, they are not the same flame, and, in another sense, they are the same, since both the first and the second have been fed from the same lamp with the same oil and both have lighted the same place. Do you believe that the interval during which the lamp has been extinguished has any relation to the fact that it is or is not the same flame?

"In the same way, a man who feels, thinks, and acts like you, who even bears the name Ananda, is not you. But the child that you once were, the pupil, the youthful seducer of

Kapilavastu, the student, and now today my disciple, different as these may be, have always been and are you.

"This means that continuity alone represents personality. Personality does not reside in matter but in your sensations and in your thought, in the combination of elements that are peculiar to you. From one life to the next, from one flame to the next, identity persists—always the same and yet always changeable."

Sometimes he stopped on the road to drink a bowl of sheep's milk.

"I am happy," the shepherd would say, "to spend my life leading my flock."

"Did you hear that?" the Blessed One would comment. " 'I' . . . Could I explain to him that the 'I' does not exist? Or could I tell him how the 'I' and the 'non-I' do exist but can be neither grasped nor separated? I would only have upset his simple mind."

Recalling that, the evening before, Maudgalyayana had lavished care on a soldier of Magadha who had been wounded in a skirmish with the frontier guards of Kosala (border incidents occurred even in those days), he took advantage of this to clarify the meaning of his words and of his silences.

"If, before the wounded man was treated, he had said to you, 'I don't want you to bind up my leg before I know who wounded me, whether he was a noble, or a property holder, or a common man, whether he was tall or short, and what wood his bow was made of. And, before any treatment, I also want to know your name and to know what plants you gathered to make this poultice for me,' what would have happened? The man would have been dead, would he not, before you could have answered all his questions?

"In this way, Maudgalayana, there is no point in my telling you if the world is eternal or not, if it is infinite or not, if the vital force is like the body or differs from it, if your spirit does or does not live after death. Only perfection, if you achieve it, can teach you these things. What I have revealed to you all will be heard, but what I have passed over in silence will be kept from human ears."

Time passed, drought succeeded the rains, scarlet leaves replaced the apple blossoms, days followed nights, plains alternated with mountains and forests with rivers, people passed and paused and talked, kings nodded and Brahmans caviled—and the disciples never tired of listening to the Master. Everything offered a pretext for instruction, as every flower offers its nectar to the bee that gathers honey for the hive.

Although he had bid farewell to Kapilavastu, Shakyamuni had, nevertheless, to return to the city once again. While at Vaisali he learned that his father was so ill that the doctors and even the Brahmans versed in magic had given up all hope for the dying man. When he arrived, he found the aged sovereign bedridden and miserable, his breath short and his tongue shriveled.

"Thou hast traversed a long, long road, O King, and thou hast always striven to do right. Thou hast turned aside from evil desires. The black wings of anger and hatred have not brushed thee. Happy is he who glimpses his face in a polished silver basin, filled with clear water, and sees there no blemish. Happier still is he who knows that his heart has kept pure. Thy death is like a beautiful summer evening."

The servants, in tears, were gathered around Maha Prajapati, who had left the community to keep watch by the side of her devoted and faithful companion. Speaking with difficulty, Suddhodano took his leave. "For the wrongs I have done you, my friends, you have harbored no resentment, because you sensed that they were involuntary. And thou, my

companion, who my feeble eyes can still see art all tears, simply think of the child thou didst raise who now assures me of my salvation."

Respectfully the Master closed the old King's eyes and crossed his arms over the once vigorous chest. Then he turned to those present. "You all see the body of my father. He is no longer what he was, for nothing can conquer death, and what is born must die in order to be reborn again and again until it is delivered."

All the Buddha's enemies were not disarmed simply by meeting him. The cures that he effected—for no detail in the four arts of medicine was unknown to him—and his miracles touched hearts predisposed to purity, but they exasperated others. Some men could not countenance the people's turning from them to give their allegiance to one far more powerful.

One has to admit that the Enlightened One was not content merely to radiate peace and soothe troubled hearts. Like a true Kshatriya, he attacked the opposition, criticized false doctrines, denounced deception. It was not enough for him to stigmatize error; he treated his adversaries as hypocrites or charlatans, and the fact that these mortifying charges were often deserved only enraged them the more. "What are these outer signs of purity worth—the plaited hair, the white loincloth, the sacred cord on the chest—when the inner man is impure?" Yet, when he detected a pure heart behind the proud exterior, he sought to help it.

Such was the case of a certain Brahman who enjoyed a great reputation because he gave forth light from the hollow of his navel. The man was frightened to see his belly grow dark the instant he stood before the Perfect One. The latter explained to him that they had met in the course of a previous life.

"You even offered me a crown in the form of a crescent moon! . . . But that was a transitory deed, although the light of its glory remains with you. If you heed my doctrine, it will assure you an eternal reward."

The Brahman was overwhelmed and was forthwith converted, but his colleagues were corroded by the acid of hatred. They bribed a woman to make advances to the Buddha after he had dismissed the disciples and was preparing to sleep; then they went about the city crying that the famous wise man was far from practicing in his own life what he preached for others. Poor Sundari, who had not been able to elicit a single word or glance from the Buddha, tried to protest. She was found by the gate of the monastery, her throat slit. "No doubt," the Brahmans cried, "the impostor wanted to silence her. Let him be brought to justice!"

Wine loosens tongues and casts caution to the winds. The murderers got drunk and fell to quarreling among themselves, each claiming to have delivered the fatal blow so as to get the biggest share of the sack of money paid them by the Brahmans. The story ends, as it should, with a moral: murderers and instigators alike were held upright and buried to the waist, covered with rice chaff that was then set afire, and roasted slowly, the flames being fed only by small handfuls of fuel.

It would be a mistake, however, to believe that the simple fact of being a Brahman automatically created a feeling of mutual defiance between this superior caste and the Buddha. Many times—the irreducible Jains apart—Brahmanic religious came to listen attentively to him, questioned him, and, in good faith, bowed before his irrefutable arguments. It is enough to mention one priest who arrived from the distant city of Jevatra after spending several months in preparing his questions.

"What, Master, is the sharpest of all swords? The most

potent of all poisons? The hottest of all fires? The darkest of all nights?"

"Speech, covetousness, lust, ignorance," the Illumined One replied without hesitation.

"Good . . . good . . . And what is the best weapon? The most impenetrable armor? Also, what man enjoys the greatest gain? And who endures the heaviest loss?"

"Surely, Brahman, wisdom is the finest of all weapons, and nothing can pierce the breastplate of patience. As to profit, the man who gives without waiting to receive gains beyond compare, while he who receives without giving will lose everything."

The Brahman was both satisfied and thoughtful. He continued: "Tell me what it is that attracts and what repulses. What pain do you consider the most terrible and what satisfaction the greatest? And one more question: Who brings about the ruin of this world—the gods, the rulers, or men themselves? Who shatters amity between brothers and what fever devours them?"

"Beyond doubt, good attracts and evil repulses. Immense pain results from wrongdoing, whereas liberation from the passions pours honey and cream into the heart. As for the ruin of the world, over and above gods, kings, and men, it is caused by ignorance. And it is ignorance, in alliance with envy and egotism, that sets brother against brother; then a feverish hatred heats their blood. Is that all that you wanted to know?"

"Yes. . . . And yet I wonder still if something exists in this world tenacious enough to resist fire, wind, water, and time. . . . Powerful enough to help man build his house. Do you think that the gods—"

"The gods are the gods, Brahman, and all are good for those who honor them with a pure heart. . . . But there are, indeed, two tenacious and powerful things: the love for all that which is created, and the reward for good deeds."

Respectfully, the Brahman bowed before the Master. Returning to Jevatra, he expressed himself thus to his disciples: "I found a man who has won happiness. His Law is good and his heart profound. Without delay go and hear him speak. He has more to teach you than I."

The worst enemy of the Perfect One was Devadatta, eldest brother of Ananda and, therefore, the Master's first cousin. He, too, had donned the yellow robe, but he had not lost one jot of his pride thereby. He had worked out regulations of exceptional severity for a new sect, and these he submitted for the Buddha's judgment.

"Your instruction, my cousin, is all gentleness," Devadatta said, "and I criticize it because it does not lead to holiness, because it does not condemn the flesh. . . . The body, which is composed of thirty-two elements devoid of any divine attribute, is conceived in sin, is it not? From birth it is condemned to corruption, is it not? Being subject to pain, it is the instrument of the trials created in our previous existences. It contains within it the germs of sickness, of decay, and of death. Therefore, we must treat it as a vessel of abomination and cover it with rags scavenged from dung heaps."

"Indeed," the Tathagata replied, "the body is filled with impurities and no one questions that it must return to dust. But still, because it is the instrument of our trials, we must make it a vessel of purity, not of sin.

"It is wrong, certainly, to give oneself riotously to the pleasures of the body. But it is no better to deny the body those satisfactions that its needs demand and thereby to add fresh stains to its impurity. . . . The dirty lamp that lacks oil will go out, and the body that is tormented and consumed by mortification will be ill disposed to welcome the light. . . . No doubt, Devadatta, one cannot forbid a man's observing rigorous rules if he believes he will find the way to health

through them, but to impose such rules is so inauspicious that I will oppose your doctrine with all my strength."

Devadatta did not insist, although secretly he spat upon the Law, but he feared defeat if he were to challenge the Master directly. He changed tactics, therefore, and determined to achieve his ends obliquely. He was an extremely intelligent and energetic man; he envisaged his taking over leadership of the community as a matter of course.

"Master, you are now very old. Do you not find that governing the monks tires you? Why not hand over the direction of the community to me? Then you will be able to rest. You will be free of care and you can meditate on the divine Law you have revealed to us."

The bantering tone of the Tathagata's answer was nonetheless steely.

"I see how good you are to me. Too good, even! . . . Look! I will know when the time has come to give over direction of the community. For the present, I will continue to see to its management. And if I would not leave it even to Maudgalyayana or to Sariputra, who are truly great spirits, do you think I would entrust it to you? Devadatta, to *you*, to a man whose darkened mind sheds less light than a cracked lamp?"

He was not angry—a Buddha is freed from outbursts of passion—but he had to speak out with authority to suppress certain waverings he sensed in the order. Firmly he strode off in search of Sariputra.

"Go to every crossroad in the city and proclaim so that all can hear you; 'Beware of Devadatta! He has strayed from the right path and is lost. He is wandering in directions that lead nowhere. The Tathagata is not responsible for the words or actions of this madman. The Law no longer inspires him and the community is closed to him. Henceforth, Devadatta speaks only for himself.' "

The dangerous cousin took no apparent notice of this humiliation, but neither did he seek to submit once more to the Buddha's authority, nor did he try openly to fight the Saint whom King Bimbisara protected too closely for anyone to dare attack him. Devadatta knew that he could count for his revenge on Prince Ajatasatru, who was devoured by ambition to rule and who hated Shakyamuni.

To impress the Prince, Devadatta exploited the magical powers that he possessed; he appeared before him in the form of a little boy, with four serpents at his ankles and wrists, one twined around his neck, still another coiled on his head, and a seventh across his shoulder. Then he reassumed his normal shape as a vigorous man.

Now confident of his ascendancy over the young man, he unceasingly distilled the most pernicious notions in his ear. Playing on the Prince's impatience, he talked of how life is so short that many men who are worthy to rule are deprived of their deserved success; he dwelled on the King's inexhaustible vigor of mind and body. Every word ate like acid into the mind of Ajatasatru. Little by little, a hideous idea was implanted in his brain. He began to confer with strange characters; in the small hours of the night he wandered furtively about the halls of the palace; he questioned the servants about when the changing of the guard left the King unattended in his apartments.

Finally, Bimbisara sent for his son and demanded to know the meaning of such singular behavior. Shame suddenly struck the young man to the quick; he fell to his knees and confessed his plot to kill his father and king.

". . . So I would be king!" he gasped.

"But be king, then!" the sovereign cried. "A throne is not worth a son's enmity."

With the ascension of the new king of Magadha, a harsh

era began. Ajatasatru commenced by forbidding any man to become a monk if he was still of an age to have children. Then he forbade any care of the temple where his father had placed the nails and the hair he had begged the Buddha to give him. ("Leave me some token of yourself, so that while you are away, I and mine may keep you among us still.") He went so far as to stab with his own hand a woman who defied the royal edict and left daily a garland of fresh flowers on the gold casket containing the precious gifts.

He did much worse. Urged on by Devadatta, who kept reminding him how dangerous it could be to leave a ruler at large when his subjects did not accept his abdication, he resolved to imprison his father and to allow him such scant rations that lack of food would presently have the better of the old King's robust constitution. He confined Vaidali, the Queen Mother, to her chambers because, against his orders, she would take fruit to her husband, hiding it under her sari or in her hair.

When his father's death proved slow in coming, Ajatasatru determined to have done with it. Not daring to have Bimbisara's throat cut or to poison him, he despatched a barber-surgeon to treat the abscesses that were eating away the prisoner's legs. This man—who was none other than the executioner—slashed the feet, ankles, and calves of the suffering man so thoroughly, poured such hot oil over the wounds, and dusted them with such impure salt that infection soon carried the old man off.

It is easy to imagine what an uproar broke out, what filth was hurled at the gates of the palace. But no one in Rajagriha really rebelled. There was no doubt of its having been parricide, and nothing could prevent one mouth's murmuring the secret into the nearest ear, yet the public conscience accepted the unhappy event: the King had died, most cruelly, it was true—even most unjustly—but since another ruler now

represented the people before the gods, there was nothing to do but bow before what must certainly have been the will of the highest powers. Did they not know better than mere men what should or should not happen?

However, in his turn, Ajatasatru had a son, and when he remembered his own childhood at his father's knee and when, furthermore, he compared that loving period in his life with the precarious future, his heart was eaten by remorse. A fever struck him down, and in his delirium, he saw his father, his legs swollen and blood-smeared, smiling at him with kindly affection. The young King appealed in vain to the doctor Jivaka: Jivaka threw the pills he had brought out the window, declaring that all his science could cure only bodies, not tormented spirits. So Ajatasatru, throwing off the covers under which he lay shaking with fever, betook himself to the Bamboo Grove and collapsed at the Buddha's feet, confessing to him his own horror at the crimes he had committed.

"Your father," the Wise One said to him, after listening to him the whole night long, "your father, who was a pious, honest, and good man, has gone to be reborn among the most powerful of the gods. He sees your repentance, and long ago he forgave you. . . . And you, Ajatasatru, when you will know the Law that I am going to teach you, you will no longer suffer. Cleansed of all poison, you will then be able to give your people the happiness they expect from you."

Devadatta did not acknowledge himself beaten. His humiliated pride gave way to hatred. Before leaving Rajagriha, from which the King had publicly banished him, he tried once more to make an elephant attack the Buddha. To this end he bribed the servants to set huge Nalagiri loose in the path of the Perfect One. Now, Nalagiri was the elephant assigned to the task of crushing under his left foot the heads of prisoners condemned to death. One had only to point out the victim to him for the beast to seize the man with his trunk, lay him on the ground, and split his skull as if it were a dried nut. "Woe!" people cried, as they saw the great animal bearing down on the Wise One. "Woe! Woe! The great Monk will be killed!" But the elephant bent his front legs and kneeled before Shakyamuni, and delicately lifting an hibiscus flower from a woman's hair, he offered it respectfully to the man he should have killed.

Blind with fury, Devadatta rushed to the forest to enlist the help of a bandit. He promised that when the murder had been carried out, the bandit would receive his reward from two men who would be waiting for him near a spring that he had specified. But Devadatta ordered these two churls to kill the murderer. And farther on, he posted four bullies to finish the first two off. Then, in a wood, eight men; and in a ditch by a road, sixteen; each group had orders to massacre the preceding. But the Buddha spoke to the bandit before he had drawn his dagger; dazzled by him, the man led the Monk to the two others, who led him to the next group. Devadatta, who was lurking nearby to follow developments, presently saw pass under his nose the Monk in the yellow robe leading thirty-one men who, before throwing their daggers away, had used them to shave their heads. Now, chanting a pious hymn, they were following at the heels of Shakyamuni.

Disregarding the holiness of his cousin (he had never forgiven Gautama for having, thirty years earlier, beaten him at archery, swordplay, and horsemanship in the presence of Gopa Yasodhara, whom he desired), Devadatta resolved to entrust no one else with the liquidation of a superiority that was never found lacking. He was more than fifty years old, but he had never felt so strong or so adroit. When he came upon the Blessed One as the Monk was chatting with his disciples, he picked up a huge flint with edges that cut like razors, and aiming at the throat, he hurled the stone with all

his strength. The projectile grazed a rock, swerved, and struck Shakyamuni's foot.

"Yours is a great sin," said the Buddha, gravely, without bothering to stanch the flow of blood. "It is great because your heart is evil. It will cost you, alas, terrible punishments in your lives to come. . . . Know that your criminal efforts are useless, know that no attempt on my life can succeed. Arhat and Jina, I will die only at the appointed time."

Devadatta ended his life as he had lived it—devoured by the fires of hell. Driven from Magadha by King Ajatasatru, scornfully thrown out of Kosala by King Prasenajit, and deprived of supporters, he returned to his family's kingdom. He entered Kapilavastu furtively and by night. To avoid being recognized, he had resumed wearing the yellow robe. He went directly to the palace where Gopa Yasodhara was living in devout solitude. When she heard that a monk was asking to see her, she received him at once, never doubting that he brought a message from Siddhartha. Her joy vanished when the knave assailed her furiously: "You want news of the man whom you persist in calling husband? . . . Ah! I assure you, he doesn't even remember he ever deserted you! You are mad, woman, mad never to have understood that I am the one who has loved you passionately all my life! The time has come for you to be as cruel as he once was to you. Love me, Gopa, for I worship you, and finally you can feel avenged."

She shrank back, as if struck by lightning, white with terror and indignation. Her hair was undone, she wore neither paint nor jewels, and she had never looked more desirable. He did not even hear her cry, "Coward! Coward!" but reached out blindly to seize her by the shoulders. A terrible dizziness swept over him, and his mouth filled with blood. When he came to, Gopa had disappeared.

Ravaged by a hatred that he now knew could only be

stilled by the Saint's death, Devadatta returned secretly to Magadha. He traveled at night to avoid arrest by the guards, and entered the Bamboo Grove as the Buddha was setting straight some harebrained monks who were arguing among themselves over this or that interpretation of the sayings and the silences of the Master.

"Have you ever watched some young elephants tear a lotus from a pool? They don't bother to clean the stems and roots well by dipping and dipping them again in the water until all the mud has been washed away. They eat them just as they are, and they are surprised, later, that impurities have made them sick. Do you understand me, O monks who are unable to extract, beyond my imperfect words, the pure essence of the Law?"

Never daring to hope that he would be received, Devadatta played the role of a sinner so tortured by remorse that he could not wait to confess his blackness. Pushing aside the seated monks, he threw himself at the Buddha's feet and, with mock sobs, clasped his ankles. At the same time, he tried to scratch him with his fingernails under which he had slipped an infallible poison. The Master merely pushed him back with his big toe. A crevasse yawned behind the criminal, revealing the innermost fires of the earth. With a scream, Devadatta staggered backward and, enveloped in a sheet of flame, disappeared.

Book Seven

I

IT IS QUITE HARD TO FOLLOW THE BUDDHA IN ALL HIS COMINGS and goings, for they lasted at least forty-four years. His movements were confined, however, to the small area that forms the northeast corner of modern India—Bihar and Oudh —and southern Nepal. Pali tradition has it that Shakyamuni became two persons, one of whom went to preach in Ceylon as well. But this is merely a daring interpretation of a phrase in the Scriptures telling us, without further clarification, that "in those times an ascetic sat under a tree in order to preach there."

The Wise One and his disciples used to suspend their travels during the rainy season from June to September.

Legend claims that this was done to avoid walking on insects, which swarmed with the dampness. In actuality, the summer cloudbursts turned the roads into bogs and made it impossible to preach in the open. Nonetheless, large numbers of the faithful would come to the monastery from neighboring towns. The curious came, too, to listen and left, nagged by a feeling of uneasiness. But the Buddha was not trying primarily to enlighten the masses. He did not delude himself into believing that century-old traditions, superstition, hankering after magic, and, last but not least, subservience to the Brahmans had not walled up the understanding of the common people.

"The gods matter very little," he was content to say. "They are what we want them to be. And what a boring thing it is, after all, to recite the Vedas! . . . Listen to me. Only the man who follows the true Law will quench desire and rout ignorance. And he who will understand, too, that nothing lasts and that reality is not to be found in what our senses teach us."

It could never be claimed that the entire peninsula was stirred by a great Buddhist movement during the Master's lifetime. His preaching reached only a limited area, and even here the converts were counted only by the tens of thousands. The millions of followers cited in the "Lalita Vistara" came later; they testified to the prodigious missionary effort of Emperor Asoka, a century after the death of the Happy One.

Shakyamuni himself aimed his teachings at an elite, believing firmly that such a group must lead the masses. Indian society offered him few choices. At the bottom of the scale, the Untouchables responded to magic and miracles and dreamed of being reborn as gods, no less. The peasants were close enough to nature to sense, even if confusedly, the glorious dawning of a new concept of existence, but they were in no way capable of leadership. As for the merchants, most of them were too deeply immersed in the pursuit of profits and possessions to conceive of other values. And although he counted numerous Brahmans among his followers, the Perfect One was quite anticlerical. He did not concede the usefulness of an intermediary between man and his salvation. There remained the nobles, the caste to which he was bound by his Kshatriya blood, and it was from among them that he hoped chiefly to recruit the leaders for the great task of liberation.

In 476 B.C. Shakyamuni was nearly eighty years old. To that point, age had seemed scarcely to touch him. Vigorous, active, indefatigable, he had never feared long journeys, or sleepless nights spent in searching the profundities of the Law, or the harsh midday sun of India. And his heart had preserved the marvelous youthfulness, the freshness that only a spirit that has perceived and understood everything can grant to age.

However, on leaving Vaisali where he had gone to accept a property deeded to the brotherhood by Amrapali, a famous courtesan who had been redeemed by grace, he had to stop at the vihara of Sapala, near the little city of Bilva. He felt extremely weary, and his stomach, which had been delicate all his life, was troubling him. To Ananda, who was preparing a soothing herb drink for him, he said, "I am old. I am sallow. I feel weak. Ananda, soon I will be eighty! I drag about like a broken-down old chariot! Yet I could prolong my stay on earth for the full length of one day of Brahma, if I wanted to."

Before he could show surprise—and perhaps some disappointment—that his disciple did not answer, "Stay for the good of humanity," Mara was there to whisper in his ear: "The hour has finally come. Enter Nirvana, O Happy One!"

"No, no. I know the meaning of this hour better than

you. Three months more; then and then only will the Tathagata reach Nirvana."

Many of Shakyamuni's disciples, many companions of
his youth, and kings he had helped had already left this earth.
Maudgalyayana and Sariputra, united after life as they had
been joined in friendship during their earthly existence, had
most likely entered Nirvana or, at least, had experienced a
fortunate transmigration. Kondinya had also passed on, but
the Buddha had subsequently recognized him in a child. When
this little boy saw the Master, he spontaneously professed the
Faith and offered the Buddha a fistful of sandy earth—this
earth that had testified to the past generosities of the Tathagata and belonged to him in its totality.

"Ananda, one hundred years after I am dead, this child
will be reborn in the body of a king and his name will be
Asoka. In honor of my relics, in memory of my sermons
and the miracles that I wrought to convince the blind, he will
build as many sanctuaries as there are grains of sand in this
hand."

Kings, too, had turned to dust—Suddhodano, Bimbisara,
Pradyota, King of Udayini, Udayana, King of Kosambi. . . .
Kingdoms had suffered wars. From Rajagriha troops had
come to pillage Kosambi and Vaisali. The principality of the
Shakyas had been ravaged by Virudhaka, son of Prasenajit
and brother of Prince Jeta. To avenge his having been formerly treated as the son of a slave, he put Kapilavastu to the
torch, massacred seventy-six thousand inhabitants, and had
five hundred and fifty young nobles horribly tortured.

But new disciples, after attaining one of the degrees of
holiness conferred by the Master, left the communities to
preach peace and gentleness in the villages. The Mallas,
princely governors of the city of Kusinara, were eager to

match the sovereigns of Magadha and of Kosala who had labored so long to spread the Law. Despite the opposition of the palace Brahmans, they ordered great celebrations to be prepared to receive the "unconquered Monk who comes to pour refreshing water on brows that are hot and weary."

The Buddha did not seem to want to leave the fresh shade of the country where he was resting. He had exhibited the power people expected of him by performing a service. Effortlessly, this old man lifted an enormous boulder that had split off from the mountainside and rolled down into a stream, damming it back. He tossed it into the air and, with a single word, reduced it to dust. Then he went back to his meditations.

"A time will come when some perfidious man will ask why I came to earth in the body of a woman, and he will consider this coming imperfect. However, for the man who devotes himself to holy works, the body does not share in the impurity of birth. Out of compassion for mankind he must be born among men. . . . If he were a god, how discouraging for them! 'A god can possess holiness, happiness, perfection,' they would say, 'but how can we poor, miserable humans achieve anything like that?' "

Seeing fresh color bloom on his Master's cheeks once more, Ananda dared to say to him, "You were no doubt surprised that I did not beg you to prolong your stay on earth. But when I saw you sick, I lost all my strength and all hope of holding you back from Nirvana. But then a voice reassured me and, although I was so dizzy that I thought I would faint, I remembered that you had not yet told us what you want done about the order. . . . Surely you would not enter Nirvana without telling us that."

Some swifts flew by in wild pursuit, for it was their mating season. With the speed of an arrow, they shot through the

branches without brushing against them, and the wind stirred by their flight did not even move a leaf.

"Be as vigilant as they," replied the Buddha, pointing to the birds. "Keep control of body and mind when you walk, when you think, when, awake or asleep, you rest. . . . As for the order, what does it still want from me? I have set forth the Doctrine, and there is no point I have not explained. Is there one among you who wants to rule over the community? Then let him say so. . . . In all truth, there is no need of any leader. Let each man be his own lamp and not seek another to enlighten him. Without support, let him walk firmly, guided by his own light. Only those who, after I leave, will light their torch to seek truth, goodness, and liberation will find peace. They will be my true disciples; they will find the right way.

"For the rest, I have often said to you that nothing escapes men's censure. They criticize the man who is silent, they blame the man who speaks, they murmur and protest against what is taught them. This does not matter! Do good and let others do the talking."

Leaning his frail weight on Ananda's sturdy shoulder, he rose painfully to his feet. An exquisite smile banished the fatigue from his face.

"Let the monks continue to live on charity. Let them ask of those who have, and give, to the last grain of rice in their bowls, to those who have nothing. The gates of Nirvana will be open to him who, having sown virtues, will have reaped love. . . . Love . . . It is this that enlightens, this that shines in radiance and splendor. The stars' brilliance is not worth one-tenth of the brilliance of the moon because she receives light only to give it to us. In the same way, the religious merit a man gains by going morning, noon, and evening to offer prayers and gifts in the temple is worth less than a few moments of love truly felt in the heart."

As he was crossing the river Hiranyavati, the Happy One was tempted by the fresh water, which made his stiffened legs feel invigorated, to immerse himself waist-deep. After this dip, he had such severe pains in the back that he gave up the idea of continuing on to Kusinara, although the city was already in sight. Supported by two monks, he went to sit down between two sal trees that stood alone in the middle of a meadow. Their intertwined boughs sheltered his head. As he fell asleep, the flowers closed, the animals and the birds fell silent, the earth trembled, and both the setting sun and the crescent moon rising from the opposite horizon grew dark. When he awoke later, although the season of blooming was long past, the meadows were covered with flowers. The Master pointed to the twin trunks, and said simply, "It is here that the Buddhas who have preceded me have left their bodies. When the moment comes, I, too, will return here."

Two weeks passed, and the Blessed One seemed to recover his strength. Accordingly, he led several of his disciples to the home of a faithful follower who had often walked leagues under the hot sun to bring offerings to the monks. History, unsure of what judgment to pass on this man—whether he was imprudent, or a tool of destiny—has preserved his name: Cunda, a blacksmith, son of the dancing master of the Mallas princes.

Dazzled by the honor offered him, Cunda spurred his wife, daughters, and servants to set forth a feast for the visitors. A banquet of vegetables and fruits, as was fitting. But the sauces were prepared with such skill that, so the story goes, the rice was offered in one hundred and eight ways, each so different from the other that no guest could have said that he had twice tasted rice that day. No meat, naturally, except for the guest of honor, who agreed to eat it—and to eat only that,

leaving the other dishes for his disciples. True, it was pork, and only a Tathagata could endure such food.

Was it a piece of tainted meat? Was a poisonous herb used accidentally in preparing the sauce reserved for the Perfect One? Or was it simply that the hour had come for destiny to be accomplished? . . . Pain twisted the body of the Wise One cruelly without, however, affecting his serenity. He ordered his disciples not to disappoint their host by leaving, and he asked the blacksmith to bury the meat that remained. Then, supported by Ananda, he set out on the road that led to the two trees that would shelter his imminent agony.

It was a painful journey. Although summer was drawing to its close and the sun was already setting, there was not a breath of air. The cows in the meadows, crushed by the heat, had sought out the few trees to ruminate in their shade. The path, which zigzagged between the fields, was as burning to the foot as if it had been strewn with hot coals. Often the Perfect One had to stop to catch his breath and mop his sweaty forehead. When he reached the twin trunks, he heaved a deep sigh of relief. He begged Sundaka to lay his scarf over a stone so that he could rest his head against it. But Ananda did not find this the softest of cushions, and he folded the cloth in four and then in eight. It made the Master smile.

"Maitreya," he said, "Maitreya who will come to earth to perfect my work will also have his Ananda."

A man of low caste, noticing this old man who was so sick that all the color had drained from his face, had followed the group. Now he stepped forward, took off his cotton tunic, and spread it over the limbs of the Perfect One. Immediately, the material gave off a golden glow.

"You see, Ananda? I had a glowing color such as this when I attained Enlightenment. And as I am about to achieve Nirvana, it bathes me again."

The Blessed One judged his mission completely fulfilled,

and he saw no further reason for prolonging his earthly so-journ. Had he not completed the ten acts that permit a buddha to enter the kingdom of Non-being? He had been illumined by Perfect Knowledge, and he had consecrated three-fourths of his life to meditating on the Law. He had inculcated in his disciples the firm decision never to leave the path of Wisdom, and he had converted those who had come to him of their own free will. He had shown himself in all his glory in visions, and he had unwound the fabric of his earlier lives. Like ear-lier buddhas, he had confirmed his father and his mother in virtue, and he had performed miracles in Sravasti. He had fashioned masters who would continue his work and transmit the Doctrine to coming generations. . . .

Perhaps, had Ananda spoken . . . But the disciple kept silent.

Word had spread to Kusinara that the Wise One was dy-ing. Princes and pariahs together, wealthy merchants, beggars and warriors, sick men and men in prime health had set out at twilight on the road leading to the two trees, the crests of which one could see, from far away, bathed in a diffuse, orange light. Mysteriously alerted, the monks in the environs had left their viharas and were hastening to gather the last in-structions of the Master. En route, the travelers noticed that the apple, peach, and mango trees were bearing flowers and fruits simultaneously.

Toward midnight such a multitude had crowded into the grassy meadow that its rustling kept the Perfect One awake. These people from all walks of life were too numerous for each one to be presented, as the Buddha had been known to insist. In order not to tire the Master, Ananda bowed to the Indian custom of naming only heads of households. After ac-cepting the greeting of each and courteously replying, the Blessed One addressed them all.

"Brothers, it will not be enough for you to have seen me. You yourselves must seek the truth, you must free yourselves from the sting of pain, you must resolutely follow a hard road. Remember that a sick man can become well thanks to the virtues of the remedy and without need of a doctor. . . . He who will not obey the Law will have seen me this night in vain. But he who will live by the straight path—even if he is by many weeks of walking distant from this place tonight— he will be near me."

At a sign from Kashyapa, the crowd withdrew beyond earshot and allowed the Perfect One to sleep his last sleep on earth.

When, at dawn, the Buddha awoke to the singing of the birds that greet every new day, he felt a freshness brush across his face; it was the venerable Upanava, who was fanning him.

"Thank you, my friend, but I must ask you to withdraw. The gods wish to see me, and I must speak with my disciples once more."

His voice had regained its old strength. As the rishi Asita had prophesied eighty years before, it was like the trumpeting of an elephant and, at the same time, as sweet as the cooing of a dove. He looked lingeringly at his disciples, one by one. The yellow robes pressed about him—the old men whose feet had been torn and then hardened on the rocky path of Truth and who for thirty years and longer had plumbed every subtlety of the Master's thought, and the young men, still confused and not wholly detached from the world.

All the early ones were there—at least, all those whose mission did not detain them far from Kusinara or whom death had not led to rebirth in a kingdom of joy where suffering is no more. There was Malunkyaputta, Sudarika, Kapathika, Sagata. . . . Kashyapa now governed the order by virtue of the authority granted him by the Perfect One, who had also charged him to codify the regulations for monastic life. In

token of his esteem for Kashyapa's vigorous mind, the Master had bequeathed him his own robe, now worn, faded by the rains, and consumed by the sun. And when the disciple took the cloth in his hands, it had immediately seemed to be shot through with threads of gold.

"Take this humble robe, Kashyapa," the Blessed One had said. "Take it. When the time comes for you to fall into the sleep of great peace, you will cover yourself with this, and you will lie down on the side of this mountain. The earth will open under you and will enclose your rest. . . . And much later, a bodhisattva will send an earthly reflection here to live his last existence, as I have done, and to be enlightened. His name will be Maitreya, and he will be born into a family of Brahmans. He, too, will acquire Supreme Knowledge in a meditation, here on this very mountain. Then the earth will open again, and you will awaken to hand on the robe of investiture to this new Enlightened One. . . . But all of this will come to pass in far distant days, thousands and thousands of years from now."

Now the hour had come to formulate his final instructions.

"Enter, O monks, on the path. There you will find no hate, which causes pain equal to that of passion, nor will you find the desolate fraud of sensuality. Be compassionate, and hinder no man, be he infamous or despicable, on the path of his elevation. Give and receive generously, but take no man's goods from him.

"The divining arts of foretelling good and evil are forbidden to you. Seek neither wealth nor comfort, but, nonetheless, eat to appease your hunger, drink to quench your thirst, and satisfy your bodily needs. Subdue, however, the fires of sex and flee from women, for they will make you lose sight of the light of the spirit.

"Practice the profound meditation to which I have accustomed you, struggle firmly against sin in yourselves, and check it gently in the faithful. Oppose the sacrifice of animals. Everyone is able to take life, but no one can give it. It is a marvelous gift, worthy of respect in the smallest creature. If the seven lights of wisdom illumine your spirit, you will in this way put an end to your painful rebirths.

"Know, O monks, that these are my last teachings. I exhort you and I say to you: all that is complex and compounded must be broken up; all that lives must grow old and die. You see this now in the body of the Tathagata! Seek beyond illusions for that which is eternal."

Suddenly, the face of the Blessed One froze. Ananda thought he had turned to marble and groaned, "Oh, how much I have still to discipline myself! I am so far from the goal, and here I am, soon to be without a master."

"After all that I have taught you, how can you still feel pain! . . . Is it so hard, then, for a man to be quit of suffering? Ah! The child is right to cry at birth; he knows already that existence is a long agony, that it is nothing but pain."

There was a ring of weariness in his voice as he spoke of the difficulties men experience in struggling to rid themselves of dross. Then he went on, "Death is an evil that strikes terror to the hearts of all creatures, but this evil is caused only by ignorance. . . . How weak and miserable is man! He believes that the great problem of the world is death, forgetting that the great problem is Life! Death at the end of a virtuous and reflective life is its supreme solution; it leads to peace. Only evil men suffer because the burden of their karma has been increased and they are obliged to be endlessly reborn in this world of evil and pain."

The questions Ananda suddenly found to ask were so numerous that they buzzed inside his head like hornets imprisoned in a glass jar filled with honeyed water. He managed only to inquire, "Which places shall we venerate, Master, to honor you when you will no longer be with us?"

"Truly, Ananda, only one—your heart . . . But since men require landmarks, I will indicate four.

"The first is Lumbini, where I was born. Let those who will be going there evoke the youth of Siddhartha.

"The second is the Bo Tree of Buddh Gaya, at the spot where, during the four vigils of a single night, Gautama was enlightened with Knowledge and came to understand the laws of the universe.

"The third is Benares; it was in the Deer Park that I met my first five disciples and that I set forth for them the Noble Eightfold Path. With them I shared the bowl of milk that a shepherd, seeing we were not Brahmans, offered us without fear of defiling our bodies.

"The fourth and last is this stone between these two trees. Here the faithful will be able to say, 'The Tathagata has fled from the world, delivered of every tie. He has risen forever into Nirvana.' "

It had been written that up until the last moment the Buddha would try to bring salvation to a man. The man who appeared at this moment was a beggar called Subhadra. Not a religious, not an ascetic whose rations come to him because those who give wish to perform a meritorious action that will bring them a reward. This was a poor wretch, lazy, sly, and a little drunk, too. Once he had been a Brahman, and for many years he had played on the compassion and apprehensiveness of others: "Have pity, good people. Just think, fate could have made you as miserable as I!" And he would exhibit his vermin and his scurvy until the woman he was importuning, happy in her health and her possessions, would fill the outstretched begging bowl and slip in a coin or two as well.

As Subhadra drew near, protesting loudly that the doubt created in his mind by certain sectarian leaders would give way to faith if the Blessed One spoke just one word to him, Ananda wanted to drive him away. But the Wise One raised his hand.

"Let this man come. . . . Countless are those who, like Subhadra, want to see and to hear so that, later, they may decide to believe. . . . Come here, you. Time is pressing, and although the rule provides that you should be a novice for at least four months, I accept you among my monks."

The day was advancing. The air grew leaden, presaging a thunderstorm. The flies were buzzing maddeningly, and the birds had taken refuge in the woods. Seeing that his disciples were following the approach of death on his countenance, the Buddha found the strength to sit up unaided, and crossed his legs in the lotus position. His hand raised in token of argumentation, he asked them:

"Perhaps you thought that if my word was stilled, you would be without a Master? . . . Well!" he continued, as their anxious silence gave him his answer, "well, it will not be so. I will not regain my strength, for the time has come. But when Shakyamuni dies, the Buddha remains with you.

"Let truth and the rules of the order stand in place of a master for you. You have four times seven religious duties to respect.

"Be mindful not to parade your good works; not to gossip; not to slumber to excess; not to show sectarian spirit; not to nourish unhealthy desires; not to take pleasure in unworthy company; not to let yourselves be distracted from your meditations.

"Believe in the Law; be modest, reserved, desirous of learning the many things you do not yet know, courageous, thoughtful.

"Exert yourselves to attain wisdom by developing memory, and through study of the Doctrine, intellectual vigor, liveliness of spirit, calm, attentiveness, and poise.

"Recognize the inconstancy, the unreality, the lack of holiness, and the corruption of all things; imbue yourselves with the need for renunciation, indifference to profane pleasures, and for suppressing the germs of evil.

"Do not forget, moreover, that you must submit to the six other duties of good society. In public or in private, be agreeable to your fellow disciples in action, word, and thought. Practice charity, moral conduct, and lead a fraternal life in the faith that leads to blessedness."

His temper wavered slightly when Ananda asked him how the monks should treat his remains.

"That's no business for monks," he growled. "There are enough Kshatriyas, Sudras, and Vaisyas to take care of my funeral ceremonies. Let them treat me like a Master of the World, like a Shakravartin."

The sun was sinking to the horizon, a blazing purple, and those present thought that they saw in a cloud the radiant image of the red Amitabha, Jina of the West, the Infinite Light. The Buddha's glance suddenly kindled, and his eyes glowed with a kind of ecstasy.

"If you know the causes of suffering, if you obey the Law, if you follow the Eightfold Path, do not think that you do these things because you are awed by the Master of creatures who live enclosed in ignorance as in an egg. It is I who have been the first to break the shell; I have been the one guide for your hearts."

Then, in a sudden easy movement he lay down on his side, his head turned to the north. He looked one last time at the group that, with hands pressed palm to palm, would accompany him in thought. The keenest ear scarcely heard him murmur, "Come, monks. What can give peace and light, this I have told you. As for the rest, if I have not taught you, why let it worry you? . . . I can repeat to you only this: never forget that every created being is subject to destruction and that the one Truth is eternal. Work tirelessly toward your own salvation."

These were the last words of the Buddha, spoken in such a smothered voice that even echo could not sound them back again. Night had fallen; the trees, like ghosts, raised toward heaven branches from which all blossoms had just fallen. A crushing silence hung over the earth. As the Tathagata passed from one degree to the next in the four stages of meditation, a golden light, growing more and more intense, enveloped his body and restored to him the youthfulness of a man of forty.

When the moon waned, Ananda placed his hand on the throat of the Blessed One and, trembling, he confided in a low voice to Anurud-sha, "I believe the Master is no longer breathing.

"No, Ananda, our Lord has reached the point where all awareness is quenched."

For a week the earth did not leave off panting; the sky was streaked with strange glimmerings, the wind bore the lamentations from the paradise of the Thirty-three to mingle with the mourning of men. Twenty-four times the image of the Delivered One was projected against the clouds.

He, the wandering monk who was born and who died like a man among men, had a funeral worthy of the greatest king India has ever known. For eight days, garlands of flowers were fetched from Kusinara to Pava to adorn the surroundings. Tents were set up for the faithful, who crowded in without distinction of caste. The palace musicians came to accompany the songs that honored the cremation.

Naturally, the monks allowed no one the task of wrapping the body of their Master in a cloth of snow-white cotton.

Then they swathed him in five hundred bands of finest muslin before laying him in a coffin of gold, which they sealed after filling it with a scented oil. It was necessary to wait to transport the body until the kings had chosen the site where it would be given to the destroying flames. It cannot be said definitely that the cremation actually took place on the banks of the holy Ganges. The only thing recorded for us is that, after a long delay, a gigantic pyre of sandalwood was raised at a crossroads in the presence of all the gods, the disciples, men from every country in the peninsula, and even animals. Custom required, in fact, that cremation and the raising of a tumulus for a king or a saint should take place at a crossing of roads leading to the four cardinal points.

Prodigious things happened in the course of the cremation. Seven times the Mallas princes thrust a torch between the dry branches, but the wood refused to catch fire. Only when Kashyapa seized the torch and, without approaching the bier, bowed low before the feet of the Master did a hundred tongues of fire leap up tall and bright. The new monk Subhadra, in his intoxication, tried to shout, "Death has at last delivered us of the ascetic prince. Now we can . . ." and here he was struck dumb. The fire died out instantly, once its work was done. The musicians did not have to support the children's voices; a heavenly choir that sounded from everywhere and nowhere, the plucking of harps, and the sweet melodies of flutes reduced the performers to silence. The delicate scent of jasmine suffused the air.

For eight days the ashes were honored in Kusinara, where they had been placed in the House of the Nobles, under a cupola of lances and bows crossed in homage to the warrior who had been the Sage of the Shakyas. However, war nearly broke out over the question of who among the several kings would keep the remains of the Perfect One. Orders went out

for the war elephants to be painted and the battle chariots to be fitted with the curving scimitars. Archers were stationed on the walls of the rival cities.

It was the Brahman Drohna who found the peaceful formula. He divided the ashes into eight equal parts and presented a golden urn to Ajatasatru of Magadha, to the Licchavis of Vaisali, to the Shakyas of Kapilavastu, to the Bullis of Allahappa, to the Kodyas of Ramagramma, to the Mallas of Pava. The seventh fell to the Brahman Vathadvipa. The Moryas of Pippalivana, who arrived late for the ceremony, claimed the eighth urn, but Drohna shook his head.

"I can give you only the ashes of the wood that burned the earthly body of the Tathagata. In return for keeping the relics, I have asked the kings and the Brahman to whom I have entrusted them, to build seven stupas, each to be forty times as high as the length of a man's arm from elbow to finger tip. The eighth urn is given into the care of the seven-headed Nagas who keep watch in the heart of the pathless forest."